Owl Magick

Explore Our Fascinating Connections with These Birds Through Folklore and Magickal Traditions

Rieka Moonsong

ROCK
POINT

Dedication

This book is, as always, dedicated to my children, Hailey and Jake. You will always be the greatest thing I have ever done. I am so proud of you both and love you so much.

Contents

Prologue

Step out into the night, where darkness reigns and the shadows creep into every corner, erasing the memory of the Sun that dared to brighten the path in the light of day. The ghosts of the forest seem to lurk behind every tree. The Moon begins to rise, offering some guidance but also deepening the shadows, hiding what needs to be seen, appearing seemingly forever out of reach. The sounds of the night surround you: the croak of the bullfrog, the song of the crickets, and then . . . the unmistakable hoot of a lone owl.

Do not fear the night, for it is here in the shadows, within the darkness, that some of the greatest wisdom lies. The owl hoots again, begging you to follow her call. Find her perched on a thick branch just overhead as she looks down at you with wide and knowing eyes, peering into your soul.

Looking back at her, you can see the ancient wisdom she carries within those eyes. She says another soft hoot and you hear her message: there is much work to be done, and she is the path to uncovering the wisdom and knowledge that has been hidden away deep within your own soul over many lifetimes. As she preens herself, a single feather drifts down and right into your palm: a gift and a reminder of this encounter.

Rieka Moonsong

Introduction

Hello and merry meet. I am delighted that this book has made its way into your life; perhaps the owl has been speaking to you and now you are ready to learn their magick. Or maybe you have always loved owls and are curious about how they can help you in your magickal practice.

As a born witch and Shaman, I have worked with many different animal energies over the years, including the energy of the owl. My personal owl guide is a beautiful snowy owl that came to work with me over a decade ago. Connecting with animal energy and magick is one of my gifts, and it is my hope that through this book, you too will learn the beautiful significance that owls have in our lives, as well as how to easily connect with them so that they may assist you in your magickal practice.

Within these pages, you will gain insight into the wisdom and magick of the owl. Linking documented facts about this bird of prey to some of their metaphysical qualities will give you an understanding of how their magick works and why. You will learn about myths, legends, and superstitions, as well as the history of cultures that venerated and persecuted the owl.

Owls are powerful messengers and guides. This book will teach you how to interact with the raptor in these roles as well as when they come to you as a familiar. Learn how to receive messages from them and how to bring their magick into your practice with spells, rituals, and meditations. Learn how to incorporate found items such as feathers to enhance your magick, as well as how the different energetic makeups of various owl species can be put to use.

At the end of the book, you will find a reference section with the magickal tools mentioned throughout to help you better understand them and be able to work with them in relation to owl magick. If you need to look up any of these tools, please refer to page 138 at any time.

For those who are new to witchcraft and working with magick, note that invocations and spells are two different things: an invocation only calls the energy to you, while a spell incorporates that energy into your magickal working. Also keep in mind that rituals tend to be longer and more ceremonial in nature than a simple spell, calling in different aspects of magick to work with for your intended purpose. Because they are more tedious than a quick circle cast and incantation, rituals aren't something you would want to do in a pinch. However, they can be a wonderful option for deep-seated issues that may need a little more work, such as trauma and concerns surrounding familial or societal conditioning. Some spells and rituals will call upon you to use a candle and work with fire; please remember to use caution when working with lighters, fire, candles, or anything of the sort.

On Silent Wings They Fly

The magickal and mysterious owl holds the key to ancient wisdom, flying silently through the night with messages from the gods.

O wls are the oldest known non-fowl land birds. Paleontological evidence shows that they were present between 60 and 57 million years ago. With their ancient lineage, it is no wonder that they hold such wisdom and knowledge. They are natural keepers of time and history. Their biological makeup lends itself to powerful metaphysical abilities including forging a connection with higher realms and aligning the owl with multiple deities. Because of the owl's ancient past, they have a long, rich history and plenty of stories of their prowess. Within this chapter, you will learn the history, myths, and folklore behind this mysterious creature to better understand their importance in your life and your magickal practice.

⸿ —— OWL FACTS —— ⸼

A bird of prey, or raptor, is any bird that hunts and feeds on other animals. The word raptor comes from the Latin word *rapio*, which means "to seize or take by force." Raptors include birds such as the hawk, the eagle, and yes, the owl. Owls feed on various animals depending on the size of the bird. Their prey might include mice, rats, rabbits, frogs, lizards, and snakes. Some owls have even adapted to hunt fish from the water.

Because of their predation on rodents, owls have been encouraged to nest in areas that have issues with pesky mice or rats. When an owl is not present in an area, people often resort to getting fake owls to deter rodents from gardens or areas where there is concern for mice or rats nesting. You might have seen these plastic or resin owls in the garden section of home improvement stores or your local plant nursery. The problem with these imposters is that they could deter the real deal from hunting in that area.

In the following section, you'll learn some facts about owls to keep in your arsenal.

⸿ —— Owl Anatomy —— ⸼

Owls have evolved to hunt at the time when their prey is active: at night. While these nocturnal raptors are not the only bird able to fly in the dark, they are the only bird of prey to effectively hunt at night. Most birds of prey have eyes on the sides of their head, but owls have large, forward-facing eyes. In fact, the eyes of an owl are disproportionately large compared to their skull and have evolved into fixed tubes, creating farsighted, binocular vision. This gives the owl its superb night vision, allowing them to hunt with only the light of the Moon. It also lends to their capability of seeing at a distance in the dark. The disadvantage is that they cannot clearly see close-up, and, because their eyes are fixed in their sockets, they cannot move them. Instead, owls have the ability to rotate their head and neck up to 270 degrees.

These biological adaptations give the owl a metaphysical edge when it comes to hunting down answers or desires. Its nocturnal nature and ability to see in the dark will bring power to Moon magick and enhance the vision of those that are open to working with the owl. The sharp talons of a raptor, used to capture and hold prey, have the magickal ability to help seize the moment or even ideas, as well as to hang on to them.

It has been said that, unless an owl calls out during flight, you will never hear them circling above. In general, owls have large feathers compared to other birds, with a velvety covering that helps absorb noise while flying.[1] This is particularly advantageous when it comes to not alerting prey to their presence. When silence and stealth are needed, calling upon the silent flight of the owl will be beneficial.

Invocation for Silence and Stealth

Use this invocation when you need to move silently and with stealth.

Oh, great owl,
I call to you right now.
Wrap me in your wings
With feathers made for silence.
I ask you to guide my way.
Help me with this task.
For your stealth of you, I ask.

Owl Pellets

Like all birds of prey, owls produce pellets that include any animal material that they cannot digest, such as bone and fur. However, owls tend to have larger pellets than other raptors, which contain more complete skeletons. This is because owls typically consume their prey whole, and their stomach acid is not as potent as other raptors'.[2] This adaptation leads to the magickal ability to let go of the things that are not serving you. Just as the owl compacts the unusable parts of their meal into the pellet to get rid of them, you can also tidy up the things that need to be released into something manageable.

Arboreal and Terrestrial

While you may default to the image of the arboreal owl roosting in a tree, there are burrowing owls that make their homes within holes dug into the Earth. These terrestrial owls are happy to take over the tunnels dug out by animals such as prairie dogs and voles. While tree-dwelling owls hunt the forest and the fields from above, burrowing owls often make meals of the animals that dwell within the tunnels: small mammals, larger insects such as grasshoppers, beetles, scorpions, and centipedes. Find more on these types of owls in The Magick of the Species chapter (pages 89).

℀ OWLS AND THE GODS ℀

The vibrational energy of the owl gives them access to the higher realms and, through that, powerful magick. Like other highly magickal animals, they have an association with gods across different pantheons. Owls were revered as messengers and for the energies that followed in their wake. Calling upon them was often viewed as a line of communication to the deity they represented. If you begin working with owl energy, don't be surprised if a deity associated with them takes an interest in you.

℀ Athena and Minerva ℀

In ancient Greece, the owl's hoot was recognized as "fanfare" and was an omen of protection and guidance, as well as a sign of good fortune.[3] The owl is associated with Athena, the Greek goddess of wisdom, strategy, and war. This goddess is often seen in works of art with an owl perched on her shoulder or flying nearby. Some myths say that the owl sat upon her shoulder so that it could reveal the truths of the world to her. One of her ancient epithets is "Glaukopis," which derives from the Greek word *glaux*, meaning "little owl."[3]

To honor the goddess for which the modern-day capital city of Greece was named, one side of the ancient Anthenian drachma coin, issued in 479 B.C., has a depiction of an owl. Some believe it might also be a reminder to be wise with your money.

For Greek soldiers, if an owl was spotted flying through the camp, it was seen as a blessing to fight from their war goddess, Athena. During the battle and subsequent victory of Agathocles of Syracuse over the Carthaginians in 310 B.C., owls that were seen prior to the war were viewed as not only motivation and a blessing, but a positive omen as well.[3]

Athena's Roman counterpart, Minerva, also holds the owl as her sacred animal. Minerva is the goddess of wisdom, healing, and the arts. The Romans used depictions of the owl to ward off the evil eye. And in ancient Roman belief, the owl also signified wisdom and knowledge, discernment, and culture.[4]

Due to their association with the goddesses, the owl is a powerful ally when it comes to gaining insight and working through problems. They can be called upon to help you retain knowledge, especially when needed for recall, such as during an exam. The owl can and will help you uncover knowledge your soul has retained from previous lives.

Because both Athena and Minerva were called upon to assist with strategy to win a battle, the owl can also assist with this in your life. Situations of this nature might include legal proceedings, a big game, vying for a new job or promotion, or even the battles we have within ourselves.

Spell to Gain/Retain Wisdom and Knowledge

Use this spell to call upon the owl of Athena when you need to access or retain wisdom and knowledge.

YOU WILL NEED

- A purple candle (or a purple owl-shaped candle, if you can find one)
- Lighter and matches

THE WORKING

1. Go into your sacred space.
2. Place the candle on your altar.
3. Cast a circle.
4. If you feel called to do so, invoke the goddess Athena.
5. Light the purple candle and then intone the following three times:

> *Owl of wisdom,*
> *Owl of knowledge,*
> *From your perch*
> *Upon Athena's shoulder*
> *I call to you.*
> *I ask of you that I learn*
> *The answers to the questions*
> *That I am seeking,*
> *Whether from the books*
> *Or from the higher realms.*
> *And as long as it is needed,*
> *The wisdom and knowledge*
> *That I gain, with me it shall remain.*

6. After the third intonation, end by saying, "So mote it be."
7. Thank the owl for their assistance and bid them farewell.
8. If Athena was called, thank her for her assistance and bid her farewell.

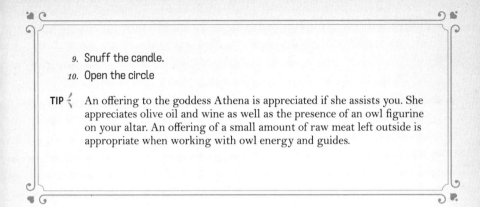

9. Snuff the candle.

10. Open the circle

TIP An offering to the goddess Athena is appreciated if she assists you. She appreciates olive oil and wine as well as the presence of an owl figurine on your altar. An offering of a small amount of raw meat left outside is appropriate when working with owl energy and guides.

Hekate

Another Greek goddess, Hekate, also has ties to the magickal owl. Although the sacred animal most commonly associated with her is the dog, she is also depicted with the owl for several reasons. Hekate is the goddess of the crossroads and, with the light of her torch, can see in all directions as well as the past, present, and future. The farsightedness of the owl aligns with this characteristic.[5]

Spell for a Strategy to Win

Use this spell when you need the owl of Athena to help you find the best strategy for a positive outcome.

YOU WILL NEED

- A red candle
- Lighter or matches

THE WORKING

1. Go into your sacred space.
2. Place the candle on your altar.
3. Cast a circle.
4. If you feel called to do so, invoke the goddess Athena.
5. Light the red candle and intone the following three times:

> *Oh, wise owl,*
> *Help me to see*
> *For the battle in front of me*
> *The plans that need to be made.*
> *Through the chaos I easily wade*
> *Show me the ways to win.*
> *My positive outcome shall begin!*

6. After the third intonation, end by saying, "So mote it be."
7. Thank the owl for their assistance and bid them farewell.
8. If Athena was called, thank her for her assistance and bid her farewell.
9. Snuff the candle.
10. Open the circle.

TIP Remember that owls love meat offerings after assisting you. Olive oil or wine are good offerings to the goddess Athena if she is called.

Hekate is also known as a dark goddess (not to be confused with evil). She is of the night and the Moon, with the ability to travel in the hidden realms. Like the goddess, the owl rules the night, hunting in the light of the silver moonbeams. Hekate is also the goddess of the witches and the keeper of keys. The keys of Hekate can be used to unlock wisdom and knowledge within ourselves as well as the world around us. Scholars believe that wisdom is the key to unlocking the world. The keys of Hekate can also be used to access portals and unlock the gates between realms and to the realm of death.

The owl's association with this dark goddess automatically ties them to witches and witchcraft. The owl is also known for being able to travel between these liminal spaces and has often been viewed as a harbinger of death. Remember that "death" does not always mean that of the physical body. It can be metaphysical or the death of things that need to cease, such as toxic relationships or certain behavior patterns.

⌔ Lakshmi ⌕

The Hindu goddess of wealth and good fortune is most often seen riding upon her sacred elephant. However, she has also been depicted riding on an owl. Myths also portray her as having an owl for a guide as they symbolize the search for knowledge that can be found within the darkness. Great wisdom and knowledge are viewed as a form of abundance and prosperity in the Hindu religion, so they are associated with the goddess Lakshmi and the owl.[6]

⸺ Spell to See into the Dark ⸺

Use this spell to call upon the owl of Hekate to light up what needs to be seen that is currently in the dark.

YOU WILL NEED

- A black candle
- A white candle
- Lighter or matches
- A journal
- A pen or pencil

THE WORKING

1. Go into your sacred space.
2. Place the candles on your altar.
3. Cast a circle.
4. If you feel called to do so, invoke the goddess Hekate.
5. Light the black candle first and intone the following:

> *Owl of Hekate*
> *With eyes wide and all-seeing,*
> *I ask you for your vision*
> *To help me to peer into the dark.*
> *Fly with me now*
> *From the pitch black of night.*

6. Light the white candle and intone the following:

> *From the shadows and into the light,*
> *Offering me your sight.*
> *Please show me now*
> *What was once in the dark*
> *Now brought into the light.*
> *So mote it be.*

7. Take a moment to see what is revealed. What comes into focus for you? Write it down in your journal in case there is work to be done around what is shown to you.

8. Ask the owl if they can offer wisdom on how to work with the issue if necessary.
9. Once you are done, thank the owl for their assistance and bid them farewell.
10. If Hekate was invoked, thank her for her assistance and bid her farewell.
11. Snuff the candles.
12. Open the circle.

TIP ⸕ Remember that owls love meat offerings after assisting you. Appropriate offerings to Hekate are keys, crossroads dirt, and dog hair. Crossroads dirt is soil found where paths or roads intersect, such as at a three-way or four-way intersection. The dirt collected from the center of this intersection is considered the most powerful crossroads dirt.

═══ Ritual to Unlock the Hidden ═══

Use this ritual to call upon the owl of Hekate when you need assistance with unlocking things that have been hidden away.

NOTE ⟨ This is a form of shadow work, so proceed with caution and know that it could unlock things that are unpleasant such as trauma that has been repressed. Please seek help or guidance from a professional if this ritual brings up any traumas that need to be dealt with.

YOU WILL NEED

- A gray or black candle
- Lighter or matches
- A timer (using your phone is acceptable)
- A journal
- A pen or pencil

THE WORKING

1. Go into your sacred space.
2. Place the candle on your altar.
3. Cast a circle.
4. Light the candle and intone the following:

> *Owl of Hekate,*
> *Show me the way*
> *Locked away and hidden*
> *But no longer is forbidden.*
> *I have your key*
> *And ask to see*
> *What it is I have blocked.*
> *Turn the key, now unlocked*
> *With owl beside me*
> *As I will, so mote it be.*

5. Let go of any preconceived ideas about what you might find.

6. Set the timer for 10 to 15 minutes and close your eyes.
7. When the timer goes off, come back to the here and now. Wiggle your toes and fingers.
8. When you are ready, open your eyes.
9. Take a moment to write down your experience—what you saw or any messages that came through.
10. Thank the owl for their assistance and bid them farewell.
11. Snuff the candle.
12. Open the circle.

TIP { Remember that owls love meat offerings after assisting you. Appropriate offerings to Hekate are keys, crossroads dirt, and dog hair.

Ragana

Another goddess of the witches is Ragana. Worship of Ragana is believed to date back to Neolithic times. She is a Baltic Moon goddess of women, fertility, and childbirth prevalent in Lithuanian and Latvian folklore. Her name is derived from the verb *regeti*, from the ancient Latvian language, which means "to know, see, and foresee."[7] With her powers of vision and ability to see into the "other," she is linked to the owl. Before the goddess became demonized, she was known as a powerful healer and guide that could lead you into the world of "other." Many stories also tell of her ability to shapeshift into a bird, often taking flight as an owl to patrol the night skies, swooping down on unsuspecting men that would dare to harm a lady.

It is believed that Ragana's ties to the night, powers of premonition, and patronage of women are what eventually linked her to witches and, through that association, forever tied owls to witches as well, thus associating them with evil.

Spell for Fertility

Use this spell to call upon the owl of Ragana when you are in need of fertility assistance. Remember that this does not just mean fertility for childbearing. It could be tied to the fertility of your land or even to creating a fertile environment in which your intentions, dreams, and desires can manifest, come to life, and grow to fruition.

TIP If you are working this for your own fertility, place your hands upon the area of your womb while you intone. If it is for your land or your garden, you can do this spell outside with your hands on the Earth, making sure the candle is in a safe place so as not to catch anything on fire. If you want to manifest your dreams/desires, write them out on a small strip of paper beforehand. Bury the paper on your property along with any offerings. Don't worry—the paper will easily biodegrade in the soil.

Remember that owls love meat offerings after assisting you. Appropriate offerings for Ragana are eggs, women's hair, and items found in nature. She also loves images or figurines of toads and frogs.

YOU WILL NEED

- A green candle (a green owl-shaped candle would be especially powerful)
- Lighter or matches

THE WORKING

1. Go into your sacred space.
2. Place the candle on your altar.
3. Cast a circle.

4. If you feel called to do so, invoke the goddess Ragana.
5. Light the green candle and intone the following three times:

Owl of Ragana
Perched within your tree
Full of life and vitality,
Please lend fertility
To grow these seeds for me.

6. After the third intonation, end by saying, "So mote it be."
7. Thank the owl for their assistance and bid them farewell.
8. If Ragana was called, thank her for her assistance and bid her farewell.
9. Snuff the candle.
10. Open the circle.

Lilith

Lilith is sometimes viewed as the primordial she-demon, but others depict her as having achieved goddess-like status. She is a prominent figure in ancient Hebrew mythology who was created alongside Adam as his first wife. She was then cast out of the Garden of Eden because she refused to be subservient to her husband. Her banishment led her to be considered ill-kept company of those that were righteous. However, many modern women look to and incorporate her energy as a symbol of their feminine rights and the feminist movement.

In the Hebrew language, Lilith, or Lilit, translates to "night creature," "night monster," "night hag," and "screech owl."[8] This translation of her name led to her being called evil and a demon mother. The ancient carving known as the Burney relief, circa 1800 B.C., depicts a goddess with wings and taloned owl feet accompanied by two owls, one on each side of her. While some scholars argue that the relief depicts either the goddess Ereshkigal or Inanna, others believe the image to be that of the goddess or primordial she-demon that Lilith became after being cast out of Eden.[8] Because of her demonization and ties to the owl and the night hag, she too is connected to witches.

Invocation to Help You Stand Up for Yourself

Use this invocation to call upon the owl of Lilith when you need help standing up for yourself. This could be within a workplace where those in authority treat you poorly, or around domestic issues, toxic relationships, or other situations where you have previously lacked the courage to stand up for yourself.

> *Owls that fly with Lilith,*
> *I invoke thee.*
> *Please give me strength*
> *And the courage to make them see*
> *I shall no longer be treated poorly.*
> *Setting boundaries, now be aware*
> *I stand in my power, wanting what is fair.*

OWL MYTHS AND FOLKLORE AROUND THE WORLD

The magick of owls is not just associated with deities, but is also recognized for the power that the raptors themselves bring, both good and bad. For many cultures, the energy of the owl was that of good fortune and assurance of wise guidance. Strange tales regarding owls come from all over the world. From messengers to carriers of souls of the departed, owls are featured prominently throughout historical legends. Some of these tales relate to owls in general, while others feature a specific species.

United States

In the United States, it was once believed that if you hear an owl cry, you must return the call or else take off an item of clothing and put it on again inside out to ensure that evil spirits stay away. In Louisiana, the Cajun culture believed that if you hear an owl calling late at night, you must turn your left shoe upside down to avoid disaster. Killing an owl in Illinois means that revenge will be sought upon your family. In Hawaii, the owl is part of their old war chants.[9]

For the Indigenous peoples of America, the owl held great magick and mystical powers. The Pima in the Southwest believed that placing an owl feather in the hand of one that was about to pass would let the owl know they were ready to make the journey; then the owl would assist with the transition into the afterlife.[11] The Ojibwa people, specifically, call the bridge that departed souls must cross the Owl Bridge.[8]

The Cherokee believed that the great horned owl, the screech owl, and the barred owl could all communicate directly with their Shamans, and their medicine men were often granted the ability to

⸻ Ritual to Communicate with the Ancestors ⸻

Use this spell when you need to communicate with those of your lineage that are in the Beyond.

YOU WILL NEED

- A journal
- A pen or pencil
- Something to carve a candle with
- Two black candles
- One white candle
- Lighter or matches
- A cauldron or fireproof dish
- A timer (using your phone is acceptable)
- If you feel comfortable with blood magick, you will need an alcohol swab and something sterile to prick your finger with. This is not dark magick.

THE WORKING

1. Write down as many names as you know or can find of deceased grandparents, second-great and so on, from both maternal and paternal sides. Aunts, uncles, and cousins are not necessary.
2. Go into your sacred space, taking your list of names with you.
3. Cast a circle.
4. Carve your mother's maiden name into one of the black candles and set it on the left side of the working space.
5. Carve your father's last name into the other black candle and set it on the right side of the working space.
6. Place the white candle in the center of the working space.
7. Light the white candle.
8. Intone the following three times:

> *Owl of wisdom, owl of ancient,*
> *I ask that you connect me with my lineage.*
> *To those that came before me,*
> *Without you I wouldn't be.*
> *To my ancestors I do call,*
> *From owl's beak, your messages fall.*

9. Light the left black candle first, then the right one.
10. Read aloud the names of the ancestors on your list.
11. Only if you are comfortable with blood magick: Swab your finger with alcohol and prick it with the sterile instrument. Wipe a smear of blood on the list of names. Swab your finger again.
12. State the following intentions of protection:

> *I will only be contacted by those ancestors that are working for my best and highest good. My circle and the owl are my protectors.*

13. Intone the following three times:

> *Blood of my blood, I call to you*
> *With owl here to help us commune.*
> *I seek your guidance and wisdom*
> *From the Beyond, let the message come.*

14. Carefully light the paper on fire, first from the left candle and then the right, and place in the cauldron to burn. (Remember to be careful using fire.)
15. Once the paper has burned, set the timer for 10 minutes.
16. Close your eyes and let your defenses drop.
17. Listen with your heart, your soul, and your blood. Let the messages, wisdom, and guidance from your ancestors come through.
18. When the timer goes off, give yourself a moment to ground and center.
19. Open your eyes and write down anything that you received.
20. Thank your ancestors for their assistance.
21. Thank the owl for their assistance and bid them farewell.
22. Snuff the candles.
23. Open the circle.

TIP Remember to give the owl an offering for their assistance. You may also give offerings to your ancestors. These are typically tobacco, dried flowers, or rosemary (for remembrance).

shapeshift into owls. This is one of the reasons that the Cherokee word, skili, means both witch and great horned owl.[12]

The Lenape believed that dreaming of an owl meant that they now had one as a guardian, and the Dakota Hidatsa revered the owl as a protector of their warriors.[8]

Some Indigenous tribes from the Americas believed that an owl in the area was actually an embodied spirit or connected to a spirit, maybe even a deceased ancestor coming to share wisdom.[13] Indigenous peoples revered their ancestors for their great wisdom, and therefore also venerated the owl. The belief that owls can reside in liminal spaces and travel between the world of the living and that of Spirit makes them a powerful ally when it comes to communication between the two. If you need assistance to communicate with your ancestors, the owl can lend a wing.

Across the Globe

Cultures all over the world incorporate the owl and its magick into their myths and legends. The folklore surrounding this bird is vast, and in many places, the power of the owl still remains mystical and magickal.

In Africa, a large owl that repeatedly comes to the area means that a powerful Shaman lives there. The Bantu of Central Africa believe the owl to be the familiar of wizards, and the Zulu people in the south believe the owl is a sorcerer's bird that brings messages of wizards and witches.[15]

In Afghanistan, it was the owl that gave man flint and iron to make fire. In Babylon, women that wore owl amulets would be protected in childbirth.[15] The owl is also a guardian of the Underworld (not the same as what some consider Hell), and a protector of the dead. Owl hieroglyphics are commonplace within the tombs.[16]

To the Celtic people, the goddess Arianrhod could shapeshift into an owl and would bring solace and healing to those that would seek her. They also believed that the owl represented the Crone goddess, Cailleach, and her infinite wisdom.[9]

In Japan, the Ainu people held the northern eagle owl sacred as a mediator between the gods and themselves, delivering divine messages and those from their ancestors. A toast to the owl would be made for good fortune before leaving on a hunting expedition. Eagle owls were often carved into their houses to ward off famine and pestilence. They also believed that the screech owl warns of danger.[9]

Owls are tied to the Underworld in many cultures and are often viewed as carriers of the souls of the departed. This holds true in Egypt, ancient Celtic lands, across many areas of Asia, and amongst many of the Indigenous tribes of the Americas. The Aboriginal people of Australia believe that owls represent the soul of women and are to be revered, for when their mother or sister passes, the owl will carry their soul away to the Beyond.[9]

For some across the Middle East, owl are the souls of people that died and remain unavenged.[11]

Because the owl is associated with the Underworld and the souls of the dead, they have become tied to witches and those that practice magick. Much like other highly magickal creatures, the owl is recognized for their spiritual attributes and how their energy can contribute to our witchcraft practices. The wisdom and power of the owl is known across the world and is held in high regard.

Out of the Darkness They Came

*Like a demon out of the darkness of hell,
the owl stalks the night skies in search of their prey.*

With so many examples of how owls are revered and associated with various deities, it can be hard to understand how they are also viewed as irrevocably evil harbingers of death and destruction. The hatred and persecution of owls and those associated with them is just as widespread as their veneration.

For every person that sees the owl as a symbol of wisdom and good fortune, there is one that believes they are a bad omen. Cultures across the world fear the owl. In many places across the world, owls are killed simply because they are believed to be evil or house an evil spirit.

HARBINGERS OF DEATH AND EVIL OMENS

In the Middle East, owls are omens of destruction and death—evil spirits that can carry away your child in the dark of night. Seeing an owl before a battle ensures that there will be many lives lost. The hoot of an owl in the morning forewarns of a bad day. Those that like to complain are associated with the owl. In Israel, the owl is considered to be "unclean" and represents desolation and blindness. [8]

In areas of Southern India, fortunes, both good and bad, were determined by the number of owl hoots that were heard. These bad omens ranged from loss of fortune to illness, mental distress, and impending or sudden death.[15]

While some African areas viewed the owl's association with sorcery as positive, others did not. In Cameroon, located in West Africa, the people believe that the owl is too evil to be named; instead, it is referred to as "the bird that makes you afraid."[15] And in East Africa, the illnesses that affect children are believed to be brought by the owl.[9] In areas of Madagascar, owls are believed to join evil witches to dance on the grave of the dead, and their hoot is akin to necromancy, said to help witches raise the dead.

Many European countries including Italy, Poland, Russia, Germany, and Hungary all view the owl as a harbinger of ill omens, including death, and if one hears its hoot, then it is potentially signaling sickness or even your own demise.[16] It was the owls that reportedly foretold the death of Julius Caesar.[17] In the Shetland Isles, if an owl flies over a herd of cattle and startles them, the female cows will give bloody milk.[18]

Early European settlers believed the screech owl was a sign of impending illness or death. Children were taught to never answer nor imitate the call of a screech owl.[10] The barn owl was known as "the bird of doom" in English folklore.[15] It is believed that both the screech owl and the barn owl became associated with the banshee because their high-pitched, keening screech sounds like the shrieking banshee.[28] The banshee is a female spirit in Gaelic mythology that when heard, her keening, screeching, or wailing is foretelling an impending death. Because she is a harbinger of death, the banshee is linked to witches in some Celtic mythology, as both are powerful, female supernatural beings that predict death or bring bad omens. The banshee, or Bean Sidhe, is of the darker Fae, and there have been stories that witches were born from the coupling of a dark Sidhe and a mortal and then sold their souls to evil forces to gain power.

⸺ OWLS AND WITCHES ⸺

This raptor has been tied to witches for centuries and part of that begins with their name. *Strix* is a genus of owl species in the Strigidae family. The Latin word *strix* means both "owl" and "witch." Despite the Roman mythology of their wise goddess Minerva and her sacred owl, the myth of the harpy often rang louder.

The ancient harpy was a predatory creature with the legs and wings of a raptor and the torso of a woman. The harpy myth gave way to stories of large owls that fed on human flesh and blood. The Romans did not feel that owls were natural and instead believed that they were witches that had transformed to fly about, wreak havoc, and spread disease and death.[15] Strix, striga, or striges came to mean a witch that transforms into a screech owl at night.[14] It is still accepted as a word for "witch" in the modern Italian language.[13]

Remember that Hekate and Ragana are known to be goddesses of witches and witchcraft, and they both have associations with owls.

Both of these goddesses are considered "dark goddesses." "Dark" in this sense does not mean evil or associated with dark magicks, but that they are aligned with some of the more taboo aspects of life, such as death or the Underworld. Because of owls' association with these goddesses, they have long been viewed as one of the animals to rule Samhain, or "Halloween" to non-witch folk.

Their nocturnal nature also contributes to the idea that witches can easily transform into owls to explore the night sky, especially on All Hallow's Eve. Along with cats, the owl quickly became known as "the witch's familiar."

BLACK MAGICK AND POSSESSIONS

There are many superstitions about owls being animals of black magick. In India, the owl is prized for their use in black magick. Illegal poaching has become an extensive problem in India due to the almost never-ending list of religious myths and superstitions surrounding the owl. While the owl is associated with the Hindu goddess of wealth and prosperity, Lakshmi, these raptors have been part of darker rituals of sacrifice to the goddess in the hope of gaining favor with her. They have long been associated with demon rituals as well as the practice of using various parts of the owl to create hexes and cast curses.[22] It is also said that one with the knowledge can summon the eyes of an owl so that they may spy on others as the owl flies about the village. Because of this, it is possible that hundreds of owls are killed each year for black magick or sacrificial purposes.[17]

In many parts of Africa, there are two prominent beliefs: that owls are harbingers of evil and death and that they are vital to witchcraft workings. Much like in India, the witch doctors of

Africa are known for using the owl for darker magicks. According to a paper written in 2022, six African witch doctors that were interviewed had individually used owls as part of their practice to bewitch others and even admitted to mixing "owl parts with poisonous plants and a lot of magic" to try to kill someone.[23] Seventeen percent of the owls killed during the time of the study  were put down because they represent omens of disaster and death.[24] During an initiation ritual, African witch doctors are often made to mingle their blood with that of an animal. It is believed that the witch doctor gains power from the animal during this ritual. In most cases, the animal being called upon must be used as a sacrifice in order to use its blood and appease the dark magicks.[25]

Of the more sinister associations of the owl—remember that Lilith has close ties with the owl and she is considered to be "the Mother of Demons"—the early Christian church adopted the stance that the owl was a symbol of evil and demonic possession. An owl outside of someone's home might be a signal to these early Christians of demonic possession in the works.[11]

These early Christians believed that the owl, with its affinity for the darkness, was a seeker of only "vain knowledge" and was unable to perceive the divine truth. In some medieval Christian illustrations and carvings, the owl was depicted alongside the ape—a terribly evil animal that represented Satan himself. Lurking around the Tree of the Knowledge of Good and Evil in the Garden of Eden, they waited to turn other beasts away from God. The owl itself was also often depicted as Satan because, like the devil, the owl is a deceptive creature. In their selfish ways, to save themselves, owls will trick other innocent birds into becoming prey for hunters.[11]

In two different books of the Christian Bible, Leviticus and Deuteronomy, the owl is noted to be one of the "unclean" birds and therefore must not be eaten or it will taint the soul of the person.[26] The Bible also associates the owl with desolation and ruin because they were able to thrive amongst the ruins of ancient cities, feeding upon the small animals that returned to the uninhabited areas. This association also extends to the ruined cities of Babylon, Sodom, and Gomorrah, known as wicked, evil places that needed to be punished for their sinful ways. Hearing its lone hoot in these places of consequential devastation led to the owl being viewed as a symbol of sin and extreme punishment and consequences.[29]

PERSECUTION OF OWLS

NOTE ⟨ The following section may be hard to read, as owls have suffered tremendously at the hands of the humans that feared them.

Because of the widespread fear and hatred of owls, they have been persecuted and killed for simply being in the area. Much like black cats, owls have been trapped, tortured, and killed for their association with witches.

Owls across the globe have been shot on sight with arrows and bullets. If the animal didn't succumb immediately, they were left there to die, as no one would want to touch the evil creature for fear that they would be cursed or fall ill. Poisonous bait was left for rats and mice with the hope that an owl would prey upon the rodent before it died, poisoning the owl as well.

In areas where owls or owl parts were used for black magick, the owl was often tortured before being killed, as their suffering was thought to heighten their power for the dark forces to work with. This might include shearing off their wings or cutting off their feet while they were still alive. Sacrificial owls were also frequently cut and disemboweled.

While some places and cultures have changed their views on owls in a more positive way, most still believe the owl to be an evil creature or a harbinger of death and destruction. It is easy to forget that, while those of us who are able to commune with animals and feel their energy know they are inherently good because of their association with the natural elements, others still rely on ancient myths, legends, and superstitions that tell them a different story.

The Occultish Owl

Owls fly into our lives carrying a tremendous amount of power and magick in a flurry of feathers.

While their haunting call in the dark of night leaves some with feelings of fear or dread, the people that take the time to understand the energy of the owl will find an amazing creature with enormous potential for magick. Witches and Shamans that are familiar with working with the power of this animal will tell you that there is no other like them. Because of their vibrational pattern and overall energy, owls are naturally drawn to magickal people. Learning to work with this power will boost your own magick and open you to entirely new aspects of magick. Because of their innate sense of wisdom and the knowledge they hold, the owl loves to play the role of teacher.

The overall energy of the owl resonates with the third eye chakra, located in the center of the forehead, just above the brow area. The third eye chakra is what allows us to see into the "other." It is linked to our perception and facilitates clairvoyance, intuition, and spirit communication, and gives us access to higher knowledge. The owl, with eyes made for peering into the dark and keen perception, can help you develop your third eye chakra. With their energy resonating with that of the "in-between," the owl can teach their witch to see into the beyond.

While most species of owls are nocturnal, there are several that are diurnal (active during the daylight hours), lending to both light and dark energy. Like other animals, the owl holds symbolism with both positive and negative aspects. Sometimes they come to us displaying these "shadow" traits, letting us know that there are issues that need to be dealt with that are not so warm and fuzzy. The energy of the owl embraces both the light and the dark, the positive and the negative, and can show you how to do that, as well as reveal those aspects within us and help bring balance to our whole self. This could be trying to find a work/life balance or a way to manage time for others and time for yourself. It could also come in the form of shadow work if the owl comes to you with messages that have a more "negative" connotation.

If you need help finding or keeping balance in your life, the owl can show you the way.

Once an owl leaves their mother and siblings in the nest to venture out into the world, they are a relatively solitary animal. They do tend to mate for life and remain monogamous; however, members of the migratory species typically do not stick together year-round but return to the same general nesting area, coming

⸺ Spell for Balance ⸺

Use this spell to find balance with the owl.

YOU WILL NEED

- One small white candle
- One small black candle
- Lighter or matches

THE WORKING

1. Go into your sacred space.
2. Place both the white and the black candle on the altar.
3. Cast a circle and intone the folllowing:

> *Day and night*
> *Owl gives me sight*
> *So that I may see*
> *How the scale tips unevenly.*

4. Light the black candle, then the white, and hold your hands close enough to feel the warmth but not burn yourself.
5. Intone the following:

> *Dark and light*
> *Owl helps me right*
> *The scale once more*
> *Balance to restore.*

6. Hold your hands out in front of you, palms up and alternate lifting and lowering your hands as if weighing something. Repeat the incantations two more times while doing the weighing motions.
7. If something comes to you regarding what you need to bring back into balance, say it now.
8. Let the candles burn down completely, making sure all the fire is out.
9. Open the circle.
10. Keep any remaining candle wax on your altar or in your sacred space until the desired results are achieved.

together to mate and raise young. This dual energy can help us to see the importance of having our independence as well as making time to come together with those we love.

The gift of independence is important, for it is what gives us the power to spread our wings and fly. It helps us remember that we are strong individuals that can rise above a storm to find smoother air. That we can think for ourselves instead of following a flock so that we may make choices that are best for us and our path in life. You can call upon the energy of the owl to help you find the independence you need to be able to spread your wings and fly.

Invocation for Spreading Your Wings

Use this invocation to call upon the owl when you need assistance with finding your independence so that you may soar!

With wings spread wide,
No longer in fear shall I hide.
Beside Owl I take flight,
Independence in my sight,
Confident and strong,
Knowing where I belong,
With wings spread wide
To my truth I abide.

Because the energy of the owl also resonates with the realm of the mystical and magickal, it brings the influence of the unknown. Flying into the unknown can be frightening, but it doesn't have to be. There is beauty in the unknown, and the owl's energy reminds us of that. If we knew everything that was to happen, what a boring life that would be. Letting life unfold in its mystical and magickal way leads to dazzling surprises, allowing us to be captivated by what we see before us. It shows us where we need to grow and offers life lessons that help our souls evolve.

When the owl takes flight into the dark, they know not what lies far ahead but trust that they will see what they need to when they need to, letting the unknown unfold in the way it is meant to. This reminds us that we also need to take those leaps of faith so that we may uncover what the path has in store for us along the way.

METAPHYSICAL ASPECTS

The frequency of the owl's energy is such that it aligns with powerful metaphysical capabilities. Some of the owl's physical characteristics enhance their already significant magickal abilities. While it is true that different owls have varying magick, all owls can travel back and forth into the metaphysical and astral realms with ease. Their ties to magick and the world of "other" make these raptors an impressive ally when it comes to witchcraft.

The Owl and the Underworld

The owl is one with the night and darkness, and it has been irrevocably tied to the Underworld. This is not the Christian Hell, but a place where souls are ferried once they leave their physical body and the Earthly realm. This is the place of the dead where they come to rest before they choose to reincarnate. Owls are known to help guide the souls of the departed to the Underworld and assist them to see and acknowledge the wisdom they gained during their last incarnation.

Because of the owl's connections with the Underworld, or the Land of the Departed, they can guide you to your ancestral connections. How can we have access to our ancestors and their knowledge if they have already reincarnated? The owl is vital in this role. Once a soul comes to the Land of the Departed, the owl acts as a recorder of that soul and an "imprint" of them is created to be kept there so that the wisdom they acquired during their lifetime is not lost once they reincarnate. The imprint is not a degradation of their energy but an exact record of them and their soul's experiences.

Are They Really Second to the Cat?

Remember that the owl as a magickal creature is said to be second only to the cat. Some would argue that owls are just as powerful, but they can be more difficult to gain access to because they are wild animals. However, if you find that you have an owl as a guide or a familiar, you will not be disappointed in the power they can bring to you and your spell work and rituals.

Because the owl can travel into the world of "other," they hold liminal-space energy. Liminal spaces are those "in between." This allows the owl to facilitate spirit communication, be it with your ancestors, other departed souls, angels, other guides, the Universe, or deities. Having the owl act as a go-between can protect you from energies that are not beneficial to you or could even be detrimental. The owl will also act as a conduit of liminal-space energy for your own spirit communication, giving you a magickal boost to make these connections yourself. They can teach you how to travel effectively and show you ways to protect yourself while doing so. Or they may choose to fly with you and act as a protector and guide.

Being able to travel in liminal spaces may also give one the ability to pull on that energy for powerful manifesting magick. This is pulling from the void and bringing something into creation out of nothing. This craft takes time and practice to learn, but with the owl helping you, the potential is limitless.

Clairvoyance and Omniscience

With their large eyes and ability to peer into the dark with keen eyesight, the owl is given the metaphysical ability of clairvoyance, or "clear seeing." This allows images to appear in the mind's eye or actually manifest physically. Their eyes are known to help their witches see beyond this reality as well. It can be especially helpful with learning to see people's auras as well as spirits and entities. It is not uncommon for witches with the second sight to have an owl as a guide or familiar. This capability can be used in witchcraft for spells that create heightened visual sensitivity with things such as reading body language and facial expressions.

Remember from the chapter On Silent Wings They Fly (page 11) that the owl is farsighted. This gives them the magickal ability of premonition, oftentimes being able to foresee well into the future. This is one of the reasons they were feared—for predicting deaths when they suddenly appeared near someone's home. Factor in the owl's talent for rotating their head up to 270 degrees, and these combined abilities give the owl an almost omniscient power. With a simple turn of the head, owls are able to perceive more than almost any other animal in the world just because of their physical makeup. You might find calling upon the owl to be a way to view different timelines—past and future, as well as alternate timelines that may be happening alongside ours. When it comes to making difficult decisions, looking at the outcome down the road with an owl may prove to be very useful.

⸻ Owls and the Darkness ⸻

Most that practice witchcraft are not afraid to step into the darkness, to see what might lie hidden in those shadows. This is the realm of the owl, and for those that choose to do more than just wander in occasionally, this raptor sees you and will take an interest. They feel the energy that you bring and recognize that, while you are brave enough to take on whatever the darkness may hold, you also seek the wisdom and knowledge that can be found there as well. This is one of the ways that the owl might choose a witch to guide or become a familiar to.

Remember that "darkness" does not mean evil. It is simply the flip side to the light. What lurks in the darkness, in the shadows? It is the void, the place that remains hidden but holds the key to so many things that you might be seeking. It is also a place of powerful magick if one is willing to learn how to access it. The owl can show you the way. When the owl can guide you to learning how to work with the darkness, you can begin to use it to your advantage.

Because most owls thrive during the night, they have developed the metaphysical capability of manipulating the darkness. In the dark is also where many things begin, where they are created; the dark is a place of manifestation. We plant seeds into the darkness of the soil so that they may grow into the light. The owl is a powerful ally when it comes to being able to manipulate, manifest, and grow those metaphysical seeds.

Having magick that can control the dark also means a deep understanding of the shadows. Sometimes it is necessary to work within those shadows because they are one of those liminal spaces—neither dark nor light. The owl can teach us how to step into the shadow part of ourselves without fear of what it may reveal. They show us that we all have aspects within our being that are hidden, that they are neither dark nor light, and that is okay. The owl also reminds us that, while we might have darkness in our depths, we also have the light.

The dark is also a place where light is absorbed. The owl can show you how to work magick to absorb more light when it is needed. This may be particularly beneficial during the dark half of the year when we are getting less sunshine due to the shorter days. This type of magick can also help break curses and hexes by absorbing huge amounts of light into the darkness of those spells, effectively burning them up so that they no longer exist.

Owls and Lunar Magick

Because of their nocturnal nature, owls are naturally tied to the Moon and lunar magick. Much like the wisdom that the owl holds—that of the night and the lunar energy—we witches look to the Moon, her phases, and how her energy feels in various zodiac signs to help guide and teach us. Working with the owl might help you better understand the energy of the Moon while also helping the energy of the Moon better understand you.

Because both the owl and the Moon represent psychic abilities and intuition, try calling upon the owl while gazing at the Moon and ask for guidance to see what is to come. Set water out in the moonlight and ask the owl to bless it for powerful moonwater to help you grow your psychic abilities or trust your intuition.

Working with the owl can also guide you in spell timing. The phases of the Moon all hold different energies, and timing a spell or a ritual with them can make a huge difference in the amount of power you are able to wield for the working. However, sometimes the zodiac sign the Moon is in can be even more powerful than its phase. Looking to the wisdom of the owl can guide you here.

The owl can also help you to better communicate with the energies of the Moon, whether you are a seasoned practitioner or new to witchcraft. The owl can act as a go-between for you and the Moon, facilitating a translation of her energies.

CLOAKING ABILITIES

The owl has both physical and metaphysical attributes that give them the advantage of cloaking abilities. Being able to cloak yourself allows you to go unnoticed when necessary. The color and pattern of each owl's feathers are natural characteristics that facilitate hiding in plain sight. Some owls have coloring that helps them blend into their forest habitat and even make them look like tree bark. This is especially important for the nocturnal owls that roost during the day, helping to protect them while they slumber by becoming one with their background. Snowy owls, on the other hand, are diurnal and fly about during the day. Their white feathers camouflage them in their snowy, wintry landscape, protecting them and making them nearly invisible to their prey.

If you recall from the On Silent Wings They Fly chapter (page 11), the owl has feathers that allow them to fly virtually silently through the night. This stealth in flight is another way that their physical attributes help them to cloak themselves. Within the dark of night, it is hard to know what is there when you cannot see or hear it. Use the invocation for stealth on page 14 as a way to move about freely when needed.

With their metaphysical ability to manipulate darkness, owls can further hide themselves within the night. They can pull the dark up around them, using it as a cloak that light cannot penetrate. The owl can teach its witch to do the same. While this magick does not make you invisible in the literal sense, it pulls a metaphysical veil over you so that others may simply look past you. Cloaking spells can be used in times when you feel like you are being magickally attacked, protecting you so that you have time to work on putting an end to it. These spells can cloak you from spirits and entities if the need arises or serve as a method of protection while you are traveling in the astral realms. This type of magick can also work in social situations where you would rather go unnoticed.

Hearing What Cannot Be Heard

While owls do have exceptional eyesight, their hearing is better than any other animal that has ever been tested.[27] They are not only sensitive to low-volume sounds, but can hear them at an impressive distance as well. They also possess the ability to home in on the exact location of a sound. Evolutionary adaptations in their ears and the feathers around their faces make this possible.

Most owls have ears that sit asymmetrically on their heads. This allows them to hear in a more three-dimensional way, determining the direction, specific location, and height of a sound.[19] The round, disc-shaped face of the owl and facial feathers designed to funnel sounds to their ears heighten their hearing ability. These special feathers, called the facial ruff, act as a reflector for sounds, and can be manipulated by the owl at will to increase its hearing, oftentimes by as much as twenty decibels.[30] This is how the owl can successfully pinpoint its prey under the snow in the total darkness of night.

The physical attributes that give owls their exceptional hearing also contribute to their magick for hearing in the Beyond. They sense but also hear the calls of the departed, facilitating spirit communication. Owls can and will assist their witches when it comes to being able to hear messages that are coming through. They can not only feel but also hear vibrational patterns and energy. Sometimes the energy of something can speak to us in ways that might not be able to be felt. For instance, you might not feel the curse on an antique broach at first, but the owl can help you to hear it before you touch it. This type of magick might also facilitate your ability to hear others on a level that you couldn't before—a type of energetic reading that allows you to go beneath the surface of what someone is saying so that the true meaning or thoughts can be determined. This is particularly useful if you feel that you are being deceived.

⸺ OWLS AND THE FAE ⸺

Because owls can easily travel into liminal spaces and other metaphysical realms, they have no trouble when it comes to breaching the borders of Faery. They are welcome visitors that are given important roles. The owl is a known messenger of the Fae. When imminent death or important changes are on the way, the Fae send owls to warn of them. It is believed that this is how the owl became a harbinger of death for many cultures.

Owls act as the go-between and messenger for many other things when it comes to the Fae. If you have a desire to work with faeries in your magickal practice, the owl is a wonderful ally that can assist with this communication. The owl will be able to determine that your intentions are pure and can relay this to the Fae.

There are tales of faeries that disguise themselves as owls so that they may come into our realm unnoticed. This is not surprising considering that the owl is an ever-watchful forest guardian. They often relay messages into the realm of Faery about what is going on in the human world. Because owls are considered guardians of nature, they hold special status in the realm of the Fae, as nature is sacred to them. Any mistreatment of owls might bring about the wrath of the realm of Faery.

Much like cats, owls are naturally drawn to magickal people such as witches and Shamans. This is because of their innate ability to seek out similar vibrations and energy that they can work with. They are masters at matching energies and magick and gravitate to those that work the art of witchcraft.

Witches tend to work with and utilize the natural cycles of the Earth and the Moon, as does the owl. Being in tune with the ebb and flow of these energies is very attractive when it comes to the magick of the owl, making it easier to work with them on a metaphysical level. Witches and other magickal people also intentionally seek out the higher vibrational patterns, as this is where the magick lives. Those same vibrational patterns resonate with the overall energy of the owl, acting like a magnet drawing them to the witch.

Magickal people love to uncover the secrets of the how and why. We dig into astrology to understand ourselves and others better. Some study quantum physics, quantum mechanics, string theory, and chaos theory because these concepts are beginning to explain how magick works. String theory, in layperson's terms, is the theoretical physics concept that everything within our Universe and even beyond is made of tiny strings that each hold their own vibrational qualities. The vibration of the strings then interacts with the vibration of all the other strings. This concept unifies and reconciles general relativity and quantum physics. Chaos theory combines both mathematics and physics in a delicious contradiction to find patterns and make predictions from things that are inherently unpredictable. It shows us that within random, chaotic systems, we can find and pull out repetition, patterns, interconnectedness, and constant feedback loops.

We learn about crystals and herbs to use for energetic, medicinal, and magickal purposes. We study the elements and learn their energetic properties and how they contribute to our magick. Numerology studies and books on divination line our bookshelves. The owl is symbolically tied to this thirst for knowledge, so our curiosity about the world around us is another reason owls are lured to the energy of witches.

Remember that many cultures across the globe believe that witches can shapeshift into owls. We witches are linked to this bird of prey because of our connection to the Moon, the goddesses, and Divine Feminine energy. We also share ties to the Underworld and death. Some witches and most Shamans can slip easily into liminal spaces, those places "in-between," where our feathered friend travels as well. We also seek to commune with spirits, something the owl is irrevocably tied to. We choose to work with these spirits to receive messages from the departed and our ancestors, much like the owl.

Owls are known to be portal guardians, as are witches. Owls guard portals to the Underworld as well as the realm of Faery. Witches have the ability to create portals for travel or magickal purposes, and to close those that are not meant to be open. If you struggle with this, calling upon the owl for assistance will be beneficial.

Lastly, owls come to magickal people as guides, offering help along the path of life and in our spiritual and magickal practices. They also come as familiars, but remember: only a witch can have a familiar, because it is an energetic bond that only we can sustain. This bond thrives on the magick we are able to create with them.

Maggie Vandewalle

Messages on Their Wings

Heard over the rustle of leaves and the creaking of the trees, the lone hoot of an owl within the night carries messages on the wind, right to your soul.

Animals come to us witches for many different reasons, in different forms, and in different ways depending on what is needed for each individual person. Animals may come to us in a corporeal (physical) form or in spirit form. They may also appear to us in our dreams. This holds true for the magickal owl. They are known messengers of Spirit and the gods.

For someone who is new to magick and has not yet opened up to hearing the messages that animals bring in spirit form, your owl messenger or guide might be more likely to show up in a physical form to deliver the information it has to give. Sometimes a physical form is more startling so a person will take notice as opposed to dismissing them in a dream. If you hear an owl while out walking about or one appears just outside your bedroom window before bed, you will remember that experience, but you might easily forget that the owl came to you in a dream a couple of weeks ago. These raptors are highly magickal and in the same league as our feline friends when it comes to power. Owls come to us as messengers, guides, and familiars. What are the differences between these roles and how do we recognize them?

ANIMAL MESSENGERS

An animal messenger is an animal that comes to a person to specifically deliver a message from their higher self, the Universe, Spirit, their guides, their ancestors, or a deity.

These messengers can come in corporeal form, such as seeing a snake or bear on your hike or a bunny in your backyard. You might be wildly enthralled with the ferrets at the pet store or mesmerized by the shark in the local aquarium exhibit. Animal messengers can also come in spirit form in a dream or seen through one's third eye. They are merely a visitor sent to you with a message. They may be there for a minute or even a few days depending on how long it takes one to acknowledge the message or if the message is of a more complex nature.

Owls as Messengers

The sudden appearance of an owl messenger can be a reflection of something that is needed in your life. Maybe it is showing you that there is an area or topic of study that you should pursue and how that wisdom and knowledge can benefit you. It could come as a reminder that you must first gain all the facts about an upcoming decision that needs to be made before making your choice.

Owls can represent wisdom through hardship. If you have had a harrowing life experience, perhaps the owl is trying to show you what lesson can be gained from that situation. Because owls are raptors that rely on their keen eyesight, they can bring messages of trusting your intuition and knowing what you are "seeing" can be believed and trusted. Remember that we do not see with just our eyes. We see with our third eye chakra, our hearts, and our souls. Owls also remind us of the importance of looking at things from a different perspective. There is a reason why they perch above to watch their prey upon the forest floor or circle over the field many times before diving for their meal. The owl knows that perspective is the key to a successful hunt.

ANIMAL GUIDES

An animal guide is an animal that comes into one's life as a teacher, to offer guidance, support, protection, power, wisdom, and to deliver messages. They have a personal relationship with the individual.

Like messengers, animal guides can be in corporeal form or reside only in the astral or spirit realm. Animal guides stay for long periods of time, sometimes for one's entire life. They are referred to as spirit animals or totems in some cultures. They will simply be called animal guides here out of respect for other cultures and to avoid cultural appropriation.

How does one recognize an animal guide? An animal guide is often an animal that you feel deeply connected to; sometimes it is your favorite animal. Do you feel a special bond with cats, or have you always loved dolphins? Do ladybugs constantly land on you? Maybe you see a snake every time you are out hiking. Do you often dream of a particular animal? If you notice these things about an animal, wild or domestic, chances are that they are a guide for you.

Another way to confirm if a particular animal is your guide is to keep track of how and when they show up in your life. If an image of an owl pops into your head every time you are preparing to do spell work or a ritual, then they are likely your animal guide.

Owls as Animal Guides

Owls are powerful allies when they are guides to witches, especially those that recognize the significance of their magick. Like the powerful feline guide, owls can lend magick and support, help us heal, and of course, guide and teach us. Owls guide us to the wisdom and knowledge of our ancestors as well as the knowledge we hold within our souls from our previous lives. The owl reminds us that

Working to Reveal if You Have an Owl Guide

Do this working to determine if an owl really is one of your animal guides.

YOU WILL NEED

- A white candle
- Lighter and matches
- A timer (using your phone is acceptable)

THE WORKING

1. Go into your sacred space.
2. Place the candle on your altar.
3. Cast a circle.
4. Light the white candle.
5. When ready, chant the following three times:

> *I open up to the Animal World*
> *The secret of my guide unfurled*
> *So that your voice may be heard,*
> *A resounding hoot from the raptor bird.*
> *If the Owl is to be my guide*
> *I ask that you no longer hide.*

6. Continue to watch the flame of the candle.
7. Take note if you see an owl in your mind's eye. Communication could also come as the sound of their hoot.
8. If nothing shows up for you during this working, let the candle burn another 9 minutes, then snuff it out. To continue the working, relight and burn the candle for the next two nights (a total of three nights). Use the chant each time. Remember to use caution when working with fire, ensuring it is completely out each time.
9. Open the circle.

TIP Pay attention to your dreams over the next few nights to see if an owl makes an appearance there. If any of the candle remains, leave it on your altar until you are certain of the working's outcome, then dispose of it.

it is okay to be comfortable in the dark and that does not mean that the magick we create is evil. Your owl guide will remind you to be an observant listener and to pay attention to the tiny rustlings and small disturbances you sense in yourself, in others, and in your environment. They can show you the meaning and importance of being an independent thinker. Owls teach us that we need to search out our inner truths and connect with our mystical and magickal selves.

How do you know if you have an owl as a guide? It is a feeling—one that you simply know once the idea settles. Ask yourself if you have an owl as an animal guide. What feelings come up for you? You will feel the warmth of the truth of it. Sometimes people get "truth chills," which can be best described as full body goosebumps that break out as a resonation with what is true. If you feel something like this, your answer is yes. If you are left feeling nothing or do not get a clear answer from this method, you can try some spell work to reveal if the owl is one of your guides.

Once you have established that you have an owl as a guide, notice the messages coming through that are guiding your spell work or your inclination toward the use of a particular herb. They will also guide you on your path. Every spell we work, every ritual we perform, and every intention that we set is part of our path. Take note of any messages you receive about these, as this is your guide helping you to align with that path and your purpose here.

Ritual to Call Your Owl Guide to You

Use this ritual if you have indeed established that the owl is one of your guides but you are having trouble receiving their messages.

YOU WILL NEED

- A blue candle to facilitate communication (an owl-shaped candle will make this even more powerful)
- Lighter or matches

THE WORKING

1. Go into your sacred space.
2. Place the candle on your altar.
3. Cast a circle.
4. Light the blue candle.
5. When ready, chant the following three times:

   Owl guide,
   The one that is truly mine,
   I ask that you take flight
   So I may see you with my second sight.
   Your wings and talons I wish to see
   So that I may bond with thee.

6. Be still and really listen. You have already established that you have an owl guide, so be patient and wait for them to show up.
7. Once your owl guide makes their appearance, thank them for coming to you, then intone the following:

   My owl guide speaks freely.
   Your messages I now receive.
   You came to me to teach

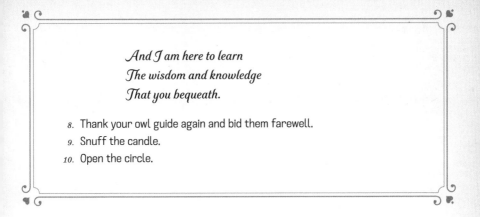

And I am here to learn
The wisdom and knowledge
That you bequeath.

8. Thank your owl guide again and bid them farewell.
9. Snuff the candle.
10. Open the circle.

Now that you have established contact and communication with your owl guide, you have to let them know that you are taking their guidance seriously. Our guides can only do so much. It is on us as the witches to follow through and do the work. Continue to notice the messages that are coming to you. Keep a journal or write things that come through for you in the notes section of your phone. This will ensure that something important is not forgotten. Also, messages are not always clear to begin with, and sometimes we only get bits and pieces at a time that have to be tied together later. Remember that if you are not completely getting what is being communicated, you can ask the owl to deliver the message or guidance in a way that you can understand.

ANIMAL FAMILIARS

A familiar is a spiritual being or entity that makes a pact with a witch to assist in their magickal workings and lend support, power, and even companionship. They can assume many forms, but animals are the most common.

Many dictionaries today still have a negative connotation for the definition of a familiar spirit. This shows us that long-held beliefs can be hard to break, even though attitudes are changing and progressing where witches and magick are concerned. While familiars are spirits or entities, they are not evil, nor are they demons, especially in the biblical sense. Familiars hold a completely different energy altogether, one that is pure magick and raw power.

The bond created with a familiar is like no other. It goes beyond the connection that one has with an animal guide. While familiars are also guides, it is important to remember that not all guides are familiars.

Familiars choose the individual that they work with, and they can also choose their form. Witches report having cats, dogs, horses, rats, snakes or other reptiles, and even birds—including owls—as their familiars. Even if a specific animal passes, it is common for a familiar spirit to come back to you in another form—reincarnation, so to speak. The familiar spirit does not die when its animal form passes over the Rainbow Bridge; it is released and may choose to return to you as another animal. The Rainbow Bridge is where our beloved pets cross into the afterlife. It is a beautiful meadow where they can play with other departed pets while they wait for their humans.

Having a familiar is a true gift. They can sit in circle with us as we work magick, lend us their power for ritual and spell work, serve as protectors and guardians, act as an anchor in this realm when we travel in the astral world, and so much more. They do all of this and can still take on the roles of guide and messenger.

Owls as Familiars

With an owl as your familiar, they can lend you an almost limitless supply of energy and power for spells and ritual work. Witches with owls as familiars might be very studious in nature and even end up as magickal or spiritual teachers. They tend to study all sorts of things but lean toward astrology and astronomy, history, archeology, and anthropology. The owl can even teach their witch about the higher areas of study such as access to the Akashic Records, where the entirety of everything that ever was has been written.

The owl will instruct their witch on the importance of going inward and the power of meditation when seeking answers. Owls are linked to the night and the Moon, so they are powerful allies when it comes to working lunar magick. Witches with owl familiars do tend to be "night owls," pun intended, and seek the quiet solace that only the darkness can provide. The owl shows their witch how to pull that night energy around them like a cloak and work with the magicks that can be found within its inky depths.

So how can you recognize your familiar? It can be harder to determine if an owl is actually your familiar as they are not an animal that is typically kept as a pet. How can you be certain that the owl that has taken up residence in the backyard tree really is your familiar? Well, like a traditional pet familiar, the bond you will feel with the owl is a bond like no other. If you have pets, take a moment to connect with their energies and feel that bond. If you have an animal guide, reach out and feel that connection—its power and how it responds to you. Now, take in the energy of your suspected owl familiar. How is it different from the others? Some describe this bond as being similar to a soulmate connection. You simply know the familiar has chosen you.

If you are still uncertain whether your resident owl is your familiar, there are several things you can do. You might consult a pendulum if you have the knowledge to work with one. If you are new to magick and it is your first time working with a pendulum, you must first figure out for yourself which movement of the pendulum means "no" and which movement means "yes" for you personally before asking it for guidance. Once you identify the movement patterns, then you can ask if you have a familiar. If the answer is affirmative and you have indeed had an owl show up recently, go into your backyard near where you typically see the owl roosting and ask if they are the familiar spirit that has chosen you. If yes, you have your answer. If not, check any other animals that you might have a connection with. If the answer for them is no, then your familiar has either not taken a corporeal form yet, or they never intend to, but will assist you from the astral or spirit realm.

Another way to reveal if you have an owl familiar is by performing the following spell. This will also help facilitate contact between you and your familiar spirit. This kind of spell working is similar to the spell work that helps to reveal if you have an owl as your animal guide.

Spell to Reveal Your Owl Familiar to You

Perform this spell if you want or need to find your familiar.

YOU WILL NEED

- A black candle
- Lighter or matches
- A timer (using your phone is acceptable)

THE WORKING

1. Go into your sacred space.
2. Place the candle on your altar.
3. Cast a circle.
4. Light the black candle.
5. Intone the following invocation three times:

> *With a brush of silent wings,*
> *Your haunting hoot in the night rings*
> *If it's truly meant to be*
> *And you are to work with me*
> *Oh, owl familiar spirit,*
> *This is my call so hear it.*
> *It is time for your reveal.*
> *Let this magick be our seal.*

6. After the third intonation, end by saying, "So mote it be."
7. Continue to watch the flame of the candle.
8. Take note if you suddenly hear the owl's hoot outside or if you see one in your mind's eye.
9. If nothing shows up for you during this working, let the candle burn another 9 minutes, then snuff it out. To continue the working, relight and burn the candle for the next two nights (a total of three nights). Use the chant each time.
10. Open the circle.

TIP Pay attention to your dreams over the next few nights to see if an owl makes an appearance there. If there are any candle remains, leave them on the altar until you're sure of the spell's outcome, then dispose of them.

GUIDES VS. FAMILIARS

We now know what guides and familiars are and how to recognize them, but how do they differ? What roles do they truly play in our lives? How can we connect with them on an energetic level? One of the main differences begins in the very definition of what they are, not only in relation to us, but also in power and overall energetic makeup. Their roles in our lives may vary depending on what it is we need them to be.

As mentioned before, guides can exist in corporeal form or solely in the astral or other metaphysical planes. One could also have a pet who has passed over the Rainbow Bridge as a guide when their spirit stays to continue to offer guidance. Familiars too can exist in the physical or metaphysical plane. While a guide spirit can choose to remain with someone for the rest of their natural life, crossing over when their person does, a familiar spirit can choose to reincarnate and come back again and again. This will be the same familiar spirit, just in a different corporeal form. Familiars can even come back in their witch's next life if they are, once again, a spiritual person, witch, Shaman, etc.

Anyone can have an animal guide, be it a cat, dog, bird, bear, wolf, lizard, dolphin, or any other animal, even if they are not aware of them. Some people even have multiple animal guides. This is especially common among spiritual/magickal peoples. However, only witches, Shamans, or other magickal people can have a familiar, and they can only have one at any given time. This does not mean that if their familiar has a physical form that passes to the Beyond that another familiar will not come to take its place. There are some stories of a person having one familiar in their younger life and then a different familiar spirit in their older life. This is not the same as the familiar spirit reincarnating in a different form. It is a completely different entity altogether. This could be an example of how the energetic or magickal needs of the witch change over time.

If you have not yet established that you have an animal guide and/or a familiar with spell work, then it is advised that you do so before trying to truly connect with them. Once the presence of a guide has been established, you can bond with them through meditations or a Lower World Shamanic journey if they do not have a corporeal form (see page 117 for the guided journey). If the guide shows up as an animal that frequents the area around your home or as a pet, talking to them or taking care of them are ways to bond with them. Speaking to them establishes that you are open to communication. Ask them questions like you might another person, such as, "How was your day?" or "Can you tell me about what was going on around here today/last night?" Don't be surprised when you start getting impressions about their feelings, images that show up in your mind, or even actual words that come into your thoughts that are not your own. This is the spirit's way of speaking with you.

While bonding with one's familiar typically involves taking care of them, this is not possible if you have an owl as a familiar. This bond will be forged and strengthened through magickal workings. The bond with a familiar that exists solely on the astral plane is also established through magickal workings. Anytime you are working a spell or doing a ritual, make your familiar aware of it. You can simply call out to them and let them know. Don't worry if they can hear you or not—they

can. They are highly magickal creatures. The more workings that can be done outside while forging this bond, the better, as this is their natural habitat. It is advised to wait until the animal reaches adulthood before consciously pulling on their magick or asking them to lend it. This is for the safety of the animal form that is the vessel for the familiar spirit, as they are still growing and that requires a significant amount of energy. If the mother owl is not your familiar but one of her hatchlings is, wait until they reach the age to be able to fly and leave the nest.

While it is more common for a familiar spirit to come to a witch in their corporeal form as a pet, remember that they can also show up as a wild animal, such as an owl, that comes and goes as they choose, syncing their appearances with Moon cycles or when magick is afoot. If this is the case, it is up to the witch to respect the boundaries set by their familiar. It is believed that familiar spirits appear as wild or stray animals when it is their first time coming out of the astral or other metaphysical realms. It is an adjustment for them to be in a physical form and they may find it difficult to stay in one place for long periods of time. You can still bond with them in the same way—taking care of them by leaving fresh water out, maybe making nesting material available, and talking to them when they are around. If you have an available area that faces where your owl has taken up residence, try creating your altar space there. You can also leave your window open while working magick.

Animal guides and familiars that exist only in the metaphysical realm can also make appearances in the physical world. This can come in the form of a seemingly random owl sighting on your porch or in the tree outside your workplace. How will you know if this is more than just a chance encounter? Open yourself up and feel it. Have you asked something of your guide or familiar recently?

Have you been seeking guidance or the answer to a problem or question? If yes, then this is more than likely their way of bringing that message or coming to your aid. Because your owl familiar or their spirit is in the form of a wild animal, you might try visiting a place where owls reside such as a local zoo or aviary. If you do and suddenly an owl is making a kerfuffle, don't discount the encounter.

Whether you have found an owl to be a messenger, guide, or familiar, know that there is a reason they have come into your life with their magick. Be still. Be open. And most importantly, listen.

Working with Owl Energy

We have all the answers we need within our souls.
Sometimes we simply need the darkness to truly see it.
The owl guides us through the dark.

The energy of the owl is wild and free. They are one with the sky, and as birds of prey, they are often viewed as more intense than their insect-eating brethren. Because of their connections to the Moon and the goddesses, owls embody Divine Feminine energy and that of the "wild woman."

If feeling wild and free is something you need, taking to the skies with the owl is just what the witch ordered. Be aware though, the Flight of the Owl Ritual on the following page is not for the faint of heart. It means flying into the darkness, into the unknown, with your wings spread wide, and trusting in your ability to see what lies ahead. The ritual requires letting go of fears and being

Flight of the Owl Ritual

Use this ritual when you feel like it's time to take flight with the owl to find the wild freedom the soul craves.

YOU WILL NEED

- A safe, comfortable place to go into a meditative state, such as your sacred space
- A white, silver, or brown candle
- Lighter or matches
- A feather of any type
- A timer (using your phone is acceptable)
- A journal (optional)
- A pen or pencil (optional)

THE WORKING

1. Go into your sacred space. Make sure you have a comfortable space set up where you won't be disturbed.
2. Place the candle and the feather on your altar or within that sacred space.
3. Cast a circle.
4. Light the candle.
5. Pick up the feather and intone the following:

> *Flight of the Owl,*
> *Please show me how.*
> *Wind over feathers,*
> *Wing to wing together.*

6. With the feather hand outstretched, turn in a circle going deosil (clockwise) three times.
7. Wave the feather overhead and then follow through down to the ground and back up again, coming to rest over your heart.

8. Intone the following:

> *I take flight with owl at my side.*
> *From the wild freedom I will not hide.*
> *Flight of the Owl*
> *Will show me how*
> *By the light of the Moon I see,*
> *As I say now, so mote it be.*

9. Let go of any preconceived notions of what might happen.
10. Set the timer for 10 minutes.
11. Prepare to fly with the owl. This will be different for everyone. You may take flight from the ground, the top of the building, or a tree branch. You might have your arms turn to wings of your own, might become an owl as well, or might stay exactly yourself alongside the owl, flying into the night sky. Remember to let go of all preconceived notions of what this is supposed to be. Take three deep breaths, relax, and close your eyes. It's time to take flight.
12. When the timer goes off, slowly come back to the here and now. Wiggle your fingers and toes, and when you are ready, open your eyes.
13. If you feel called to do so, journal about your experience.
14. Snuff the candle.
15. Close the circle.
16. Remember that you can always come back to fly with the owl.

TIP Don't worry if the flight did not happen for you this time. This simply means that it was not what you needed at this time. You can return to try again another night.

one with the moment. Sometimes this is exactly what we need, but it takes courage to intone the incantation that will set this in motion. Once you do, there's no going back; the wild freedom that is found here will change you.

WORKING WITH THE OWL AS A GUIDE

When the owl comes to you as a guide, they offer extensive access to wisdom and knowledge. Remember that animal guides also act as messengers. These messages could be something that needs to be learned or warnings of what's to come. If you are still having trouble connecting to your owl guide, refer to the Messages on Their Wings chapter (page 59) for spells that will help.

It's important to learn how your owl guide shows up for you. You might begin to receive messages from them that relate to your life path. You might also have a new awareness of your intuition. Does it seem to be on point? Or have you noticed times that you have regretted not following your intuition? The owl is showing you how important it is to trust that inner voice. It was given to you for a reason.

The owl as a guide might also lead you to become more involved with the night, study the Moon phases and constellations, learn more about the planets and astrology, begin working with lunar deities, or even look into dark goddesses.

The owl will teach you how to access more of your own psychic abilities, nurturing your intuition and insight as well as helping you to uncover any other hidden talents or abilities. It can be difficult if you feel that you are always flying blind, but with the owl's help and guidance, the unknown won't seem so daunting. When it comes to navigating the twists and turns of life, they will teach you how to do it with confidence and purpose and help you develop a deeper understanding of your own nature and the world around you.

Your owl guide will teach you to be a keen observer, and allow you to "see" with your other senses as well. They will teach you how to get a clearer picture of your environment by seeing the overall instead of what is simply obvious.

WORKING WITH THE OWL
AS A FAMILIAR

If you have not already established if you have an owl as a familiar, refer back to the Messages on Their Wings chapter on page 59 for spell work to do so. It is important to know if the owl is indeed your familiar and not just a guide before you try working with them in the higher magicks. Remember that a familiar will have access to more power and have greater abilities than that of a guide.

Once you know if an owl is your familiar, you can begin working with them on a higher level. Whether they reside in the physical or metaphysical world, work spells and rituals outside to be in their presence.

Your familiar supports you in many ways, including lending power and magick to your spells and rituals. The owl will act as a conduit of energy as pure magick flows from them and the metaphysical realm directly to you. Over time, this can strengthen your own magick greatly and could also lead to new abilities.

A familiar can and will cleanse the energetic space and even your own energy. Owl feathers in particular are wonderful for clearing heavy energies and leftover magick after spell work or rituals. If you find an owl feather while out hiking or in your backyard, this is likely a gift from your familiar. Clear your energy or that of others by waving it up and down, close to the body, in your aura.

Spell to Clear Heavy Energies

Use this spell to clear heavy energies from a space. Simply wave the feather from the ground up to as high as you can, fanning the energy toward an open door or window and intone the following:

> *By the feather of the owl*
> *I banish you now.*
> *Heavy energies are no more.*
> *Out the window, out the door.*
> *My owl and I decree*
> *As I will, so mote it be!*

Remember that the owl can help you see into the dark and beyond the veil, including the veil of illusion and deception. Being able to cut through illusions will allow you to see not only the true intentions of others, but also into your own true state of mind or what you might be hiding from yourself. The owl familiar can also facilitate the ability to peer into your past lives, allowing you to learn from them and begin to heal any traumas that may have been carried into your current life.

Your owl familiar shows you the meaning and importance of being an independent thinker. There is a time to fly with the flock and there are times when you need to fly solo. Your owl familiar will teach you the beauty of being a free thinker who is able to trust your own ideas. When this happens, it allows you to seize opportunities that might have gone unexplored before.

The owl is the keeper of Sacred Knowledge, the soul bird of antiquity. It has been said that the energy of the owl also aligns with that of Saturn, the Great Teacher. Under the guidance of an owl familiar, you become a diligent student, especially when it comes to magick. As a familiar, this raptor will show you the way into the higher levels of learning. When you are able to tap into the metaphysical realms to access knowledge, a whole new world opens up.

In the Magickal Circle

Learning how to work with your owl familiar while doing spell work or rituals can be a bit tricky, whether they are in the physical or metaphysical world. Remember that the best way to bond with your familiar is through your magickal practice. Even though working with a wild animal can seem like a daunting task, have faith in your familiar and the bond that you share. It is already there if they have chosen you—it only needs to be strengthened.

We witches know that when working magick, belief is the key. Likewise, belief in your familiar and their ability to connect with you and your magick is imperative. You must believe that when you call on them, they will be there, either physically as a wild animal or in their metaphysical form.

If you want to call your owl familiar into your magickal circle or space, they will need a place to roost. If you are working outside, this is not an issue. A simple wooden or metal chair or stepladder will make a fine perch. Use the invocation below to call them in. Once the two of you have worked together more, you may decide to write your own invocation, or your owl may give you one they would like you to use.

Invocation to Call Your Owl Familiar into the Magickal Circle

Use this invocation to call your owl familiar into your magickal circle for spell work or a ritual. Cast your circle and intone the following:

> *This is my call, please hear it.*
> *To my familiar spirit:*
> *The circle has been cast*
> *With your power vast.*
> *Owl familiar of mine,*
> *Join me in this time.*
> *I see you here, perched.*
> *There is magick to be worked.*
> *So mote it be.*

Once you are done with the working, bid your owl familiar farewell and release them from the circle. This can be done in your own words.

TIP Remember that offerings are appreciated after any working. A small amount of raw meat left outside will suffice.

MAGICKAL PROTECTOR AND GUARDIAN

One of the most important roles of a familiar is that of a magickal protector and guardian. Because the owl is closely associated with Hekate, the goddess of witches and witchcraft, these familiars excel at task. They will lend protection when you are working magick, strengthening the circle that keeps you safe. They will fend off any magickal or psychic attacks that may come your way from other individuals as well. They will also guard against anything that may want to come through from the world of Spirit that has less-than-virtuous intentions. The owl familiar can assist their witch in closing any portals that may be "leaking" negative or heavy energies. If you travel in the astral realms, your owl familiar will happily fly with you as your guardian.

Because of their ties to the night, an owl as a familiar will also protect you while you sleep. They guard not only your physical body, but your energetic one as well, for we are vulnerable while asleep. This includes magickal and psychic attacks as well as vulnerability to the world of Spirit. It is also a time when we are likely to travel about in metaphysical or astral realms unknowingly, leaving our energetic beings unprotected. If your owl familiar senses any of this, they will immediately come to your rescue.

PSYCHIC LINK AND BONDING

Between every witch and their familiar is a psychic link, and nurturing that bond is extremely beneficial for both the witch and the familiar. With an owl familiar, this is especially important because there are very limited opportunities to bond with them in a physical form. This link allows you to connect with your familiar and their energy, magick, and power in an instant should you need them.

Remember that one very direct way to grow this bond is by working with your familiar during spell work or while in ritual. The more you work with your owl, the quicker the bond and psychic link will grow. While there is no real shortcut for growing this bond, the following spell will help to strengthen the connection that is already in place.

Having an owl as your familiar is a truly unique experience—one that is a gift to be grateful for. They make excellent spiritual companions for their witches. They will lend you power and guidance for your personal life path and your magickal practice. They will give you access to wisdom and knowledge that you might not have found on your own. Continue to work with your feathered friend as much as you can so that this bond continues to grow.

Spell to Strengthen the Bond with Your Owl Familiar

Use this spell to help you strengthen the bond that you already have with your owl familiar.

YOU WILL NEED

- A white or purple candle (an owl-shaped candle in one of these colors is even better)
- Lighter and matches
- A timer (using your phone is acceptable)

THE WORKING

1. Go into your sacred space.
2. Place the candle on your altar.
3. Cast a circle.
4. Use your invocation to call your owl familiar into the circle.
5. Light the owl-shaped candle and intone the following three times:

> *The bond between familiar and witch*
> *Closer and stronger we do stitch.*
> *Through our beings it will lace,*
> *Psychic link grows into place.*
> *Of each other, becoming more aware,*
> *Magick and power we will share,*
> *Owl familiar and me,*
> *As we will, so mote it be.*

6. Feel the energy wrap around you and your owl familiar and know that the bond you share is growing.
7. Let the candle burn for at least 9 minutes or burn completely out. Make sure all fire is out entirely.
8. Thank your owl familiar for joining you and bid them farewell.
9. Open the circle.

The Magick of
the Species

They say that the magick of the owl is second only to the cat,
but have you ever seen a cat fly through the dark of night?
Or better yet, fly at all?

O wls as a whole are extremely magickal beings. They have their own power beyond that of messengers, guides, familiars, or their ties to deities. There are about 250 species of owls in the world, and they live on every continent with the exception of Antarctica.[32] While their overall energy is that of wisdom bearer and teacher, each species has its own unique metaphysical qualities as well. Sometimes that power comes from a physical attribute, and other times it comes from their habitat. "Form follows function" can be applied to the owl in the way their evolutionary physical attributes show up as a result of their habitat.

The scientific order that owls belong to is called Strigiformes. This order is broken up into two different family groups, Tytonidae and Strigidae.

TYTONIDAE

The Tytonidae family is made up of barn owls, grass owls, masked owls, and bay owls. Their heart-shaped faces make them unique and set them apart from the owls belonging to the Strigidae family.[33] Because of this special physical characteristic, they have the magickal ability of linking the heart and the mind in a powerful way so that they work together and not as separate entities.

We are often torn between following our heart and listening to what is going on in our head. Calling upon owls in the Tytonidae family can let our hearts and minds speak openly with one another so that a decision can be made for our best and highest good. The barn owl truly excels at this skill, and that is why it is called upon for the following ritual. You can learn more about this beautiful owl as well as their metaphysical properties in the Owl Feathers and Their Magick section (pages 101-106).

⸻ Heart and Mind Ritual with the Barn Owl ⸻

Work this ritual when you find the need to have your heart and mind communicate efficiently in order to make the best decision for yourself or the situation.

YOU WILL NEED

- ❦ A fireproof tray—a cookie sheet or cake pan will work well
- ❦ One yellow candle that promotes intellect and mental clarity
- ❦ One blue candle to facilitate communication
- ❦ One pink or red candle for the heart
- ❦ About 18 inches (46 cm) of natural fiber twine—cotton works well
- ❦ Scissors
- ❦ Lighter and matches
- ❦ A timer (using your phone is acceptable)

THE WORKING

1. Go into your sacred space.
2. Make sure the topmost part of your altar or working space is sitting in the northern direction.
3. Place the fireproof tray on your altar.
4. Place the yellow candle to your right inside the tray, to the east.
5. Place the blue candle in the very center of the tray, to the left of the yellow candle.
6. Place the pink or red candle to your left inside the tray, to the west.
7. Cast a circle.
8. Invoke the barn owl by intoning the following:

> *The power of the barn owl,*
> *Please hear as I call you now.*
> *Your presence to fill this space*
> *And the magick of that heart-shaped face,*
> *I ask that you join me here*
> *And help to make things clear.*

9. Take the length of twine and affix it near the top of the yellow candle. Loop the twine in a figure-eight motion from the yellow candle to the blue candle three times, staying near the top of both candles. Then, going from the blue candle, loop the twine around the pink or red candle in the same figure-eight motion three times, again, staying near the top. Tie off the twine and cut away any excess.

10. Light each candle, beginning with the yellow candle in the east.

11. Intone the following:

> *Your special magick is what I seek,*
> *Allowing my heart and mind to speak.*
> *Together they shall decide*
> *Emotion and logic, without pride.*
> *No warring between the two,*
> *Helping me see what's best to do.*
> *Barn owl perched here with me,*
> *As we will, so mote it be!*

12. Watch the candles as they burn down. As they melt, the twine will catch fire, setting the spell into motion and allowing your heart and mind to communicate efficiently. (Remember to use caution when working with fire.)

13. Once the twine has burned up, set your timer for 10 to 15 minutes.

14. If you feel comfortable, close your eyes and relax. Let go of any thoughts or preconceived ideas you have about this decision or situation. This will allow the working to do its thing.

15. When the timer goes off, wiggle your fingers and toes and open your eyes when you are ready. Ground yourself.

16. Ask yourself how you feel about the decision or the situation now. What immediately comes to you? This is the result of the heart and mind working in sync. If there is nothing immediately, don't worry. Sometimes spells take a bit of time.

17. Continue to let the candles burn down until they are completely done. Make sure all fire is out.

18. Thank the barn owl for their assistance and bid them farewell.
19. Open the circle.
20. Leave the tray with the wax remains on your altar until you are sure of what needs to be done. Once that happens, you may dispose of any remaining wax and ash into the trash.

TIP Remember that owls love offerings of raw meat (left outside) in return for their assistance.

⌒── Grass Owls ──⌒

The grass owl family includes the African grass owl, which is found in sub-Saharan regions of Africa, and the Eastern grass owl—sometimes referred to as the Australasian grass owl—found in Asia, parts of New Guinea, the Philippines, Australia, and the western Pacific. Both the African grass owl and the Eastern grass owl make their homes in grassy areas, including tall grass meadows, savannahs, and damp, swampy areas, depending on the subspecies.[34] They make excellent allies when it comes to your home lawn and its health. They can guide you on which plants work best and help with rain spells as well. Grass owls will also take to agriculture fields in search of rodents and are viewed as a friend for keeping them away from crops. They will assist you with lawn and garden pests as well.

Invocation of the Grass Owl

Use this invocation to call upon the energy of the grass owl to assist you with your home lawn or garden.

> *Grass owl, I call to you.*
> *Please fly this way.*
> *Grass owl of the savannah,*
> *Help me with my lawn.*
> *May the rains come when needed.*
> *Grass owl of the crop fields,*
> *Help me with my garden.*
> *May the pests stay away.*
> *Grass owl, I call to you.*
> *Please fly this way.*

Grass owl feathers will also aid your magick. They are generally dark to light brown in color with a white underbelly, so it's possible to find both brown and white grass owl feathers. You can find their magickal properties in the Owl Feathers and Their Magick section (pages 101-106).

⊱══ Masked Owls ══⊰

The masked owl resides in Australia and New Guinea. They prefer to live in forested areas and have been seen along timbered waterways. They also frequent open spaces on the fringe of woodland areas, especially for hunting.[35] Because masked owls call the forest home, they make excellent allies for communicating with the trees.

They get their name from the "mask" that is formed around their eyes and beak by darker colored plumage. Their heart-shaped facial disc is typically a creamy white color with a dark ring around its outside border that matches the darker shade that rims their eyes and beak. While their mask helps us to identify them, it can also help you hide your identity if the need arises. You can mask your face or even your energy.

Invocation of the Masked Owl

Use this invocation to call upon the energy of the masked owl to assist you with masking your identity or energy.

> *Masked owl, I call to you.*
> *I need to remain unseen.*
> *Whether face or energy,*
> *Please help to mask and hide*
> *What is needed at this time.*
> *Masked owl, I call to you.*

The masked owl's plumage ranges from light to dark brown and white, so like the grass owl, there is an opportunity to find both brown and white feathers. You can find their metaphysical properties in the Owl Feathers and Their Magick section (pages 101-106).

⌐═══ Bay Owls ═══⌐

The Oriental bay owl lives in southeast Asia with their primary habitat being within the dense evergreen forests. The bay owl is much smaller than their barn owl cousins and has a very distinctive U- or V-shaped face. Sightings of these birds are extremely rare, and little is known about them.[36] Because these owls live in habitats that are being threatened with deforestation, working with their energy for awareness and habitat preservation would be beneficial to both the owl and the world.

Invocation of the Bay Owl

Use this invocation to call upon the bay owl and the energy of awareness.

Bay owl, I call to you.
The places where you dwell are threatened.
We combine our energies
To help the world see
That your home needs protection.
The jungles and wild places are sacred
And Mother Earth cries out to us,
Discontinue deforestation!
Bay owl, I call to you.

STRIGIDAE

The Strigidae family includes all owls not included under Tytonidae. These owls all have round, disc-shaped faces. They vary greatly in size, with the elf owl being the smallest at 5 to 6 inches (12 to 14 cm) tall and weighing 1.2 to 1.9 ounces (35 to 55 g), and the Blakiston's fish owl being the largest, having a wingspan of 70 to 75 inches (178 to 191 cm) and weighing 6.5 to 10.1 pounds (2,948 to 4,581 g).[37] This family can be broken into two groups—burrowing owls and arboreal owls. These owls are not known for their nest-making abilities and tend to "borrow" nests by ousting the previous tenants.[10] Because this family of owls is so widespread, they have a wide range of prey depending on habitat, including rodents, fish, reptiles, amphibians, and insects.[38] Beyond their evolutionary adaptations regarding their homes, burrowing owls and arboreal owls have varying energies and magickal capabilities.

Burrowing Owls

There are twenty-two different subspecies of burrowing owls that can be found throughout the western United States, southern Canada, Florida, the Caribbean, Central America, and South America. They are relatively small compared to other owls and have longer legs in relation to their bodies than their arboreal brethren. These pint-sized raptors live in burrows underground that they either dig themselves or steal from prairie dogs, ground squirrels, or small tortoises.[39]

Burrowing owls are extremely special because they hold both earth and air energy. By making their homes within the Earth, they absorb the power of it. Their energy is very grounding and calm. Calling upon them for magickal purposes has the benefit of allowing you to "fly" yet remain grounded. This gives you access to the higher metaphysical realms as well as the ancient knowledge that is held within the layers of the Earth. Earth energy is also a powerful healer and very restorative, making burrowing owls exceptional healers.

Burrowing owls align with Sun energy because they hunt on the ground during the day. They may be willing to assist with any workings where solar magick is in play. You can also align your spell work with the time of the day that best corresponds to your desired outcome. See the Magickal Reference and Tools section on page 141 for more information.

With varied subspecies come varied habitats. The burrowing owls that live in the driest desert areas will also be imbued with that energy, while those that live on the plains or grasslands will have a slightly different energy. Through research, you can home in on the magick of the specific burrowing owl that you are calling upon.

Invocation of the Burrowing Owl

Use this invocation to call upon the healing and balancing energy of the burrowing owl.

> *Owl that burrows in the Earth,*
> *I seek your wisdom and call to you.*
> *Show me how to live in harmony*
> *And heal that which ails,*
> *Taking to the skies*
> *And walking in balance,*
> *Grounded and renewed.*

Arboreal Owls

These are the raptors that typically come to mind when you hear the word "owl." They roost among the trees, often blending in for protection while they rest during the day. They build their nests in hollowed-out parts of a tree, creating a warm, safe nook that provides shelter from the elements and protects their eggs. It is often from a branch in the dark of night that they wait for the moment to begin their hunt.

At home in the trees, these owls have a deep connection with them and often facilitate communication with the trees as well as tree spirits, also known as dryads. Tree language is unrushed, but the owl is a master when it comes to patience.

Trees and owls are very much alike when it comes to holding ancient wisdom and knowledge within them. If an owl is willing to help you communicate with the trees so they can both guide you, you should treat this as a cherished gift. Most trees have a distrust of humans—as they should—so if they are willing to speak to you and share their wisdom, it should not be taken lightly.

Invocation to Seek Tree Communication with the Owl

Use this invocation to gain the owl's assistance in speaking with the trees. This is best done while sitting beneath a tree and works even better if you are touching it, such as leaning your back against it.

> *Owl, friend of the trees,*
> *Come and join me, please.*
> *With your keen hearing*
> *This canopy finds so endearing,*
> *With patience for this task,*
> *This of you I ask:*
> *Help their words to flow to me*
> *Unhindered, true, and free.*

TIP 〈 Remember to thank both the owl and the trees. The trees will appreciate an offering of blessed water.

⌇═ Great Horned Owls ═⌇

The great horned owl is the fifth largest owl species in the world. A large female's wingspan can reach up to 5 feet (1.5 m). They are one of the most prevalent species of owls in North and South America. Their name comes from the tufts of feathers on each side of the top of their heads that resemble horns.[40] While they do not actually have horns, they hold the power of connection to the Divine and the ability to hear the soft whispers that come to us from the Universe, angels, guides, ancestors, and deities. This physical characteristic of the great horned owl is a reminder that we are connected to the Divine even if there is no physical proof.

Owls of this species are fiercely protective of their territory and nesting area. They are roughly as strong as the golden eagle which can be three or more times larger than them.[30] Their mighty strength and courage are those of a true warrior. Finding a great horned owl feather could mean that it is time to defend yourself and choose what it is you are willing to fight for.

These owls are known to be outgoing and personable. Because of this, they are frequently used as ambassador owls by nature centers and zoos to teach and promote conservation.

Invocation of the Great Horned Owl

Use this invocation to call upon the warrior-like energies of the great horned owl when you need the courage to stand up and fight.

Warrior owl of the forest,
The great horned one,
Bringing Divine connection,
Knowing when the time is right
To take flight and to fight.
Courage and wisdom
To see the battle through.

OWL FEATHERS AND THEIR MAGICK

If you are lucky enough to find an owl feather, treat it with respect because it holds the same magickal characteristics as the owl it came from. All owls have the capability of flight, giving them the power of the air element. This element is linked to the mind, intellect, the sharing of knowledge, and communication.

Spell to Bond with the Element of Air

Use this spell to strengthen the connection between yourself and the air element.

YOU WILL NEED

- A yellow candle
- A bird feather
- Lighter or matches

THE WORKING

1. Go into your sacred space.
2. Place the candle on your altar.
3. Place the feather in front of the candle.
4. Cast a circle.
5. Invoke your owl guide or familiar, if you have one, or the owl of your choice if not.
6. Once they have come into the circle, light the yellow candle and intone the following:

> *I call upon the power of the owl,*
> *Asking for help in the here and now*
> *With knowledge and communication.*
> *A bond with air begins its formation.*

7. Pick up the feather and wave it back and forth. While waving intone the following:

> *Currents of air around this feather*
> *As owl's energy bonds us together.*
> *Flowing movement, gentle and free*
> *As I will, so mote it be.*

8. Let the yellow candle burn all the way down, making sure all fire is out.
9. Thank the owl for their assistance and bid them farewell.
10. Open the circle.

If you are not someone that connects easily to this element, the owl can help you form a closer relationship with air. In doing so, you might be surprised to find that communication comes easier to you. You might also be better at accessing and retaining knowledge. Working a spell with the owl and the air element during a period of Mercury retrograde may be highly beneficial because the planet of communication and technology is ruled by the air element.

Feather magick comes in handy when working communication spells. Tied directly to the air element and facilitating a transfer of knowledge, feathers were once used for quills to write correspondences.

Owl feathers in general have many magickal purposes. Owls are wonderful allies for healing, so a feather hung in a doorway may help to keep out illnesses. These raptors are highly protective, so feathers can be kept close to ward off negative energies. And because of owls' ability to see in the dark, feathers from owls can assist you with seeing into the shadows and reveal what might be hidden. They also provide a powerful physical link to the metaphysical world and can improve your own psychic abilities. Due to the owl's association with wisdom and knowledge, keeping a feather close by might help with understanding and learning difficult subjects as well as retaining information for test taking.

Barn Owl Feathers

The barn owl is the most widespread species across the globe. While all nocturnal owls are exceptional hunters in the dark, no other animal can compete with the barn owl. This raptor can hunt in total darkness, unlike its brethren that still requires a small measure of light.[41] The barn owl utilizes their keen sense of hearing to find their prey on the darkest moonless night.[31] Because of this, their feathers offer the power to see into the dark and the unknown. If you find a barn owl feather, it could mean that it is time to find your way out of the dark you have been struggling in, and the barn owl is here to help. It may also mean that it is time to close your eyes and shut out everything else. What do you hear?

Snowy Owl Feathers

The snowy owl is the epitome of the word "adaptation" when it comes to birds. They are at home in the cold northern regions of North America, including much of Canada, Alaska, and Greenland, and migrate south in the northern United States during the winter months. They also have "snowshoes" of feathers around their feet to assist them in walking on the tundra as well as for warmth. Feathers also surround their beak area for added protection against the freezing temperatures.[42] Finding a snowy owl feather is cause to look at how you are adapting. Are you finding yourself resisting adaptation completely or have you adapted so much that you have lost yourself?

In the summer months, the snowy owl breeds in the Arctic where it's daylight 24 hours a day. This is why our snowy feathered friends hold the power of the Sun. They also hold the power of the winter. Their feathers can be helpful if you tend to lose motivation during the winter months when we have less sunlight. This does not take the place of seeking professional help if you are in crisis. However, if you find a snowy owl feather in the winter, it means that they have come to you as an ally to help you through this. The feather will help you to harness the light, warmth, and joy of the Sun.

⸻ Burrowing Owl Feathers ⸻

The feathers of burrowing owls hold the same properties and magick as the owl they come from, making them a source of air and earth energy. They can provide calm, grounding energy. Their metaphysical attributes can be found in the brown feathers. They might also have some characteristics of the spotted owl, since their feathers sometimes have white spots depending on their habitat.

⸻ Great Horned Owl Feathers ⸻

Like the burrowing owl, the feathers of the great horned owl will retain the same characteristics and magickal properties as the owl they come from. They can imbue strength, courage, protection, and camouflage. Their coloring is mostly shades of brown, but feathers can also be gray and even white.

⸻ Spotted Owl Feathers ⸻

The spotted owl, with its deep brown feathers touched with white spots and dark-colored eyes, is a representation of the light and the dark. Finding a feather from one indicates that you should search for personal truth by embracing shadow work and both the light and dark sides of yourself. These owls are also tied to old-growth forests in western North America—the places the Fae love to play. A spotted owl feather could assist you in communicating with trees and the world of Faery.

❧ Black Owl Feathers ❧

Yes, there are black owls. Although melanism in owls is a rare genetic mutation, it can be found across most of the species. Black feathers can also come from the black-banded owl and the barn owl. Finding a black owl feather means that there is work to be done within the darkness—perhaps in the unknown—such as working with divination or the world of Spirit. Black owl feathers are also extremely protective and can be used in protection spells or as talismans.

❧ Gray Owl Feathers ❧

Gray is the color of the shadows, so gray feathers will assist you with your shadow work. They are also wonderful for cloaking spells when you need to blend into the background.

❧ White Owl Feathers ❧

Any white owl feather will assist with spiritual healing. They also represent divine guidance and the power to be the light in the darkness.

❧ Brown Owl Feathers ❧

These feathers represent stability and being grounded. Finding one may assist with finding balance and stability in your life. Brown feathers are also associated with Shamanism.

If you have been blessed with an owl sighting or find one of their feathers, don't take it lightly. Owls are highly magickal birds and they come into our lives for a reason, so pay attention. Even if they are not your animal guide or familiar, these raptors have so much to teach us about ourselves and the magickal world around us.

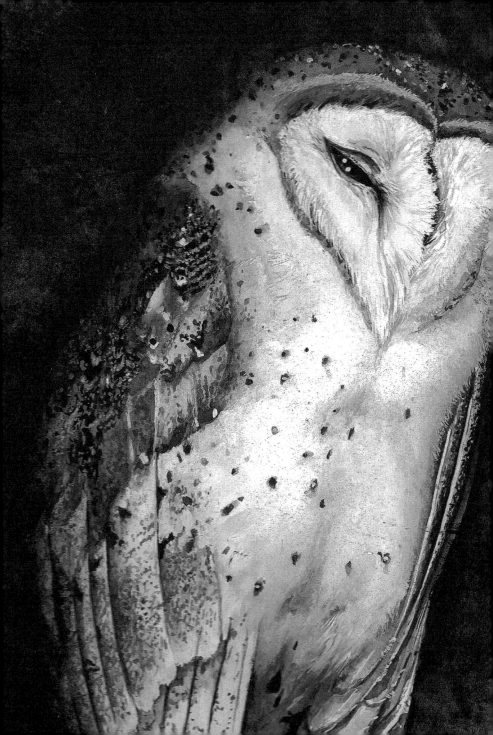

Owl Magick and Your Spiritual Practice

Owls take flight in the silver moonbeams and rule the night.

As we have learned, owls hold a tremendous amount of power and magick within them. They come to us as messengers, guides, and familiars, sharing ancient knowledge and lending support. Owls fly into our lives at just the right time, ready to teach and guide us on our spiritual and magickal journeys. When we work with their energy, it not only adds to our own. Through their wisdom and guidance, we grow and learn magickally, spiritually, and on a soul level. Taking flight with the owl as our guide or familiar can open our eyes to a world of magick that might not be possible without them. How can we incorporate this new insight into our own magickal practices?

⌁ USING FOUND ITEMS ⌁

While it might seem unpleasant at first to think about coming across owl remains, if they are treated with respect, you might find that using them in your magickal practice brings in the essence of owl magick. Many witches across the world use ethically sourced bones in their witchcraft. You might also consider finding an ethically sourced owl that has undergone taxidermy to act as a conduit for magick.

Please note that many things can be found on the black market, including owl parts, but this advice in no way supports that practice. Either find ethically sourced remains from reputable sources, or come across owl remains as a gift from them or the Universe. There are various metaphysical and occult shops as well as "curiosity" stores where you can find ethically sourced animal products. You might also consider asking a local taxidermy facility where you might be able to find what you're looking for.

⌁ Feathers ⌁

As discussed in the previous chapter, there are many uses for owl feathers, and they are the most likely owl part that you may come across. Remember that finding an owl feather should be viewed as a gift. All owl feathers can be used to help you learn to spread your wings. They cleanse heavy energies and can bring in lighter vibrations. Owl feathers also assist with psychic abilities and help one to peer into the Beyond. They are a connection to Spirit and the Divine.

Owl Talons

Like other birds of prey, the owl uses their talons to hunt. Talons also assist the owl with eating their meal while securely gripping a branch. If you happen upon owl remains or find an ethically sourced owl talon, it can be used for spells to seize the moment or opportunity. It can also be used when you need to hold on to something such as healthy habits or your money. Talons can also be used for protection magick, as the owl will attack threats using their talons first.

Owl Beaks

Owls' sharp beaks assist them in eating their meals. It is also from the beak that their call is released. Owl beaks can be used with spells for communication or for your voice to be heard. The beak is effective in making sure that what you are saying comes across as it is meant to.

Spell to Seize an Opportunity

Use this spell along with an ethically sourced owl talon to release fear and move forward boldly when a new opportunity arises.

YOU WILL NEED

- An ethically sourced owl talon or a good replica
- A red candle for courage
- Lighter or matches

THE WORKING

1. Go into your sacred space.
2. Place the owl talon and the candle on your altar.
3. Cast a circle.
4. Light the red candle.
5. Pick up the owl talon, hold it close, and intone the following:

> *Oh, mighty owl, I call to thee.*
> *An opportunity has come to me.*
> *With the power of your talons,*
> *Help me with this challenge.*
> *If this is for my highest good,*
> *Help me seize it as I should.*
> *Lend me courage and strength*
> *As I stand upon the brink,*
> *Taking flight when it's time,*
> *Grabbing hold of what should be mine.*
> *With your talons guiding me,*
> *As I will, so mote it be.*

6. Let the red candle burn out completely, making sure all fire is out.
7. Thank the owl for their assistance and bid them farewell.
8. Open the circle.
9. Keep the candle wax until you have taken hold of what is meant to be, then dispose of it.

Owl Bones

Because owls are tied to the departed and their souls, their bones can be used in spirit communication. They can be easily incorporated in the Ritual to Communicate with the Ancestors found on page 30, or can facilitate contact with other souls that have crossed over. Some might also use owl bones in divination. It is not uncommon to make rune sets from animal bones. Ethically sourced owl bones would make an excellent choice for runes since owls are irrevocably tied to the world of Spirit.

Owl Pellets

As you recall from the first chapter, owl pellets are the regurgitated bones and fur of the prey that owls cannot digest. If you are lucky enough to come across a pellet, you can certainly dissect it to use the bones it contains for magickal purposes. However, leaving it intact serves a magickal purpose as well. Owl pellets can be used in spell work or rituals where you need to let go of something that cannot serve you, especially things that can become toxic if they are not released.

NOTE As a caution, wear gloves while handling an owl pellet.

Owl Pellet Letting Go Spell

Use this spell to assist in releasing what is no longer serving your best and highest good.

YOU WILL NEED

- An owl pellet
- A small dish
- A white or black candle
- Lighter or matches
- Incense

THE WORKING

1. Go into your sacred space.
2. Place the dish and candle on your altar. Place the owl pellet inside the dish.
3. Cast a circle.
4. Invoke the owl.
5. Light the candle.
6. Pick up the dish with the pellet in it and intone the following:

> *I come here, ready now*
> *To let go and release, I vow.*
> *It has no place to stay,*
> *Out and gone away,*
> *What is no longer serving me*
> *So I may live healthily.*
> *From this I will not run.*
> *As I say, it shall be done.*

7. Hold the dish with the pellet up high and say the intonation twice more for a total of three times.
8. Set the dish back on the altar.
9. Let the candle burn down. As it does, gaze between the flame and the owl pellet, seeing whatever it is you need to let go of. Make sure all fire is out.
10. Thank the owl for their assistance and bid them farewell.
11. Open the circle.

12. Dispose of any remaining candle wax off your property. A public trash can is fine.
13. Light the incense and use its smoke to cleanse the owl pellet and the space. This ensures that the energy of the working is removed and that the working sticks. Don't leave incense burning if you plan on leaving.

JOURNEY WORK WITH THE OWL

Journey work is a practice that takes our energetic being somewhere else. This includes astral traveling, Shamanic journey work into the Upper and/or Lower Worlds, or even past life regression. The owl is a powerful ally when it comes to this type of energetic working. Because they have the ability to slip between worlds easily, owls can assist you if or when the need arises to engage in these practices.

Unlike a cat, the owl cannot act as an anchor in the physical world if you decide to travel in the astral realm. They can, however, fly with you as a guide and protector as well as see you safely back into the physical realm.

Spell to Astral Travel with the Owl

Use this spell to travel in the astral realm with the owl.

NOTE Astral travel can be done during deep meditation but is usually easier while asleep. This spell should be worked before going to bed.

YOU WILL NEED

- A mug of chamomile or lavender tea
- A purple candle
- An owl crystal or small figurine
- Lighter or matches

THE WORKING

1. Prepare and drink your mug of tea before going into your sacred space.
2. Go into your sacred space.
3. Place the candle and owl crystal/figurine on your altar.
4. Cast a circle.
5. Invoke the owl.
6. Light the purple candle.
7. Pick up the owl crystal/figurine and intone the following:

> *Into the astral*
> *I wish to travel.*
> *Guide me there without woe,*
> *With owl protecting as I go.*
> *Then see me safely home*
> *When I wish no longer to roam.*
> *Back in the physical effortlessly,*
> *As I will, so mote it be!*

8. Snuff the candle, making sure all fire is out.
9. Open the circle.
10. Place the owl crystal/figurine under your pillow.
11. Go to bed. Good night and safe travels!
12. Upon waking, thank the owl for their assistance and bid them farewell.

Shamanic Journey to the Lower World to Visit the Owls

In the Andean Shamanic tradition, the Lower World—not to be confused with the Christian Hell—is the place animal guides call home. To make this journey, I suggest recording this ahead of time and playing it back. While recording, you will want to let a silent timer run for the allotted time before the final "call back" message. It works like a guided meditation. Soft drumming in the background is often helpful. After several visits, you might find that you are able to get to the Lower World without the recording.

Find a place where you will be comfortable and won't be disturbed. Set a timer for 20 to 30 minutes to bring you back.

Take time to write down your experience or any messages that came through. Remember that you can make this journey anytime you wish.

Past Life Regression Work with the Owl

Because this magickal raptor can rotate their head up to 270 degrees and has ties to the goddess Hekate who can see in all directions, including into the distant past, the owl can easily guide you into your past lives. When we take the journey back to the lifetimes that our soul has lived before, we can gain important knowledge that we can use in our present incarnation.

It's possible to bring traumas with us into the present that were not dealt with in a past lifetime. If the trauma is severe enough, it can become etched upon our soul, requiring deep healing. By traveling back, we see how and why a trauma occurred, giving us clues as to how it needs to be healed in the here and now.

Ritual for Past Life Regression/Recall with the Owl

Use this ritual to make a journey into one or more of your past lives for learning purposes.

YOU WILL NEED

- A white or purple candle
- A lighter
- A timer (using your phone is acceptable)
- A comfortable place to sit or lie down in your sacred space
- A journal
- A pen or pencil

THE WORKING

1. Go into your sacred space.
2. Place the candle on the altar.
3. Cast a circle.
4. Invoke the owl.
5. Light the candle and intone the following:

> *Owl, creature of dark, creature of light,*
> *I wish to travel back this night.*
> *I journey to the places my soul has been;*
> *Into past lives, let me peer within*
> *All the variations that have been me.*
> *As I will, so mote it be!*

6. Set the timer for 20 to 30 minutes.
7. Sit or lie down and get comfortable.
8. Close your eyes and take three deep breaths. Let go of any preconceived ideas about what you might see on this journey.
9. When the timer calls to you, come back to the here and now. Wiggle your toes and fingers and, when you are ready, open your eyes.

10. Take time to write down what you saw or experienced. Note that not everyone sees things in images; sometimes it's an audible story that comes to you or simply a knowing.
11. If nothing came to you during the journey, that is okay too. Pay attention to your dreams and feelings over the next few days as you may receive information that way.
12. Snuff the candle, making sure all the fire is out.
13. Thank the owl for their assistance and bid them farewell.
14. Open the circle.

Not everything we encounter in past lives is bad. Sometimes, talents and gifts come through into our current life. Perhaps you were a talented artist or a skilled craftsman and you find this to be true now as well. If we happen upon a life where we were extremely happy, we can take notes from it and potentially learn how to truly make our souls happy as well. All of these things give us more insight into who we truly are, because our soul with all of its experiences is the very essence of our being.

SPELLS WITH YOUR OWL FAMILIAR, OR UTILIZING OWL ENERGY

These spells are designed to work closely with your owl guide or familiar. They can also be varied to utilize the energy of the owl if you do not have one as a guide or familiar. Remember that anyone can call upon them for guidance or assistance.

Protection Spell

Use this spell when you are in need of magickal protection. This can be used as an anticipatory set spell, or on the fly in the moment that it is needed by reciting the invocation below three times.

YOU WILL NEED

- A black candle
- Lighter or matches

THE WORKING

1. Go into your sacred space.
2. Place the candle on your altar.
3. Cast a circle.
4. Invoke the owl.
5. Light the black candle and intone the following three times:

> *To owl I call, hear my plea.*
> *Wrap your wings all around me.*
> *I feel your protection begin.*
> *No harm to come, safe within.*
> *Here I shall stay*
> *Until the threat has gone away,*
> *Over with and none.*
> *As I ask, it shall be done.*

6. Let the candle burn down completely, making sure all the fire is out.
7. Thank the owl for their assistance and their protection. Bid them farewell.
8. Open the circle.
9. Keep the remaining wax until the threat has passed and then dispose of it off your property. A public trash can is fine.

Crossing Over a Lost or Trapped Soul

Use this spell to help an earthbound soul cross into the Beyond. Light a white candle if working from home. This spell can also be used in the moment if you come across a soul that needs to be crossed.

Lost or trapped, earthbound soul,
It is time for you to go.
What ties you here abates
As owl guards the western gate.
Crossing now with ease,
May you finally be at peace.
To this the owl will see.
As we will, so mote it be.

Spirit Communication

Use this spell when you have a need or desire to speak with spirits that have departed or other types of spirits such as guides or angels. Light a purple candle when using this spell. This can also be used in the moment if you need to communicate with a spirit.

Message from the world of Spirit,
Owl brings to me so I can hear it.
In this world and that unseen
Acting as my go-between.
Words of wisdom are what I seek.
I wish now for the spirits to speak.
Their guidance I can see,
As I will, so mote it be.

One way to make it easier to connect with your familiar might be through creating a crystal grid inside the circle. Consider crystals that align with the power and characteristics of the owl, such as Moon energy, wisdom, intuition, spirit communication, and the third eye chakra. These crystals include:

- Amethyst
- Angelite
- Blue apatite
- Blue kyanite
- Blue tiger's eye
- Celestite
- Labradorite

- Lapis lazuli
- Moonstone (all varieties)
- Opal
- Selenite
- Sodalite
- Yellow quartz

You only need ten to twelve stones in total, set up using the sacred geometry method. Various geometry patterns can be used to invoke specific energies. A triangle pattern can bring balance and harmony. The circle invokes oneness. The spiral connects the physical self with the higher self. The flower of life and the seed of life are often used interchangeably and represent fertility, creativity, and interconnectedness. The most important thing is to align the crystals in a way that feels right to you in that moment.

With the owl at your side, the magick that you can work together is almost endless. Let them teach you, for it is one of their greatest roles in our lives. Perhaps someday the student will go on to become the teacher of others.

Owl Medicine

When animals bring their medicine to us, it is a true gift from the Universe. The spirit of the owl flies to us with a unique medicine all their own: an opportunity not only to heal but to learn what made us "sick" in the first place. They show us the lessons we need to learn to move forward and how to grow through our healing.

What is animal medicine? In its purest form, it is the essence of an animal that comes to us with life lessons and methods of healing for those that desire to listen and learn.[21] The "medicine" is what one gains as the animal aids in healing mind, body, and spirit.[32] Teachings have been handed down through generations of Indigenous peoples across the globe. Each Indigenous culture works with the animals that are native to their area. This does not mean that Indigenous people cannot learn the medicine from animals in other regions and countries as well. Because animal medicine is strong and powerful, it is no wonder that witches, Shamans, healers, and other magickal people seek to learn it and use it in their practices.

For many Indigenous people of the United States, the owl is part of their Medicine Wheel, taking up residence in the direction of the east, a place of illumination.[43] This is because the owl can see into the dark. Their medicine tells us that only when we go within, into our own darkness, will we receive true illumination about who we really are as a whole. With their keen vision and ability to see past illusions, the medicine of the owl lets us see reality without distortion and acknowledge it for what it is, but also reminds us that because we are magickal beings, we have the ability to alter this reality should we choose to.

This vision also offers us the medicine of not allowing others to deceive us. Sometimes we allow ourselves to be "blind" to this deception to our own detriment. Owl medicine comes to heal this and show us that we can look past what is being presented to us and choose to make the decisions that are best for us based on what we truly see.

Indigenous people across the globe see owls as consultants, and Shamans regularly seek their wisdom. Society conditions those with magickal abilities that can peer into the beyond, that what we see and feel is not "normal" and because of this, we often choose—whether consciously or not—to separate ourselves from this world. Owl medicine comes to us to heal any division or break down any walls that may have been erected between us and Spirit, the Divine, and the Universe.

As you have learned, many cultures all over the world revere the owl because of its wisdom and as the keeper of ancient knowledge. The medicine of the wise owl shows us where we should focus our studies and offers guidance on doing so more efficiently. The owl also reminds us that our souls hold sacred wisdom, and the medicine shows us how we might retrieve it. Wise owl medicine helps to heal any issues we may have with trusting our own inner voice, wisdom, and intuition.

THE OWL AS A POWER ANIMAL

A power animal is the apex of that animal's medicine. It offers the greatest lessons and healing that an animal can bestow upon us. Power animals do not ask you; they will tell you. Owls are no different. If an owl comes to you as a power animal, know that serious work is waiting for you. They will demand to be heard, but they will not simply abandon you to the work. They will guide you in what it is they have to teach you and heal you in ways you might have been unable to without their assistance.

Owls are inherently connected to the mystical and magickal. Owl power animal medicine helps you get to the root of why you might not be embracing the magickal being that you are. It heals the disconnect between you and your magick and reminds you that You Are the Magick. You might get a visit from a burrowing owl specifically because their energy resonates with the healing power of the Earth. They will help you stay calm and grounded as you work through these issues until you can find your magickal wings.

Owls show up as power animals and offer medicine to help heal your magickal vision. They show you how to see beyond what is right in front of you, not only to find the veil but to see past it to what you need to know. The barn owl, master of seeing in absolute darkness, might appear with their medicine to show you that you have never been blind to a world of magick—you just needed to be reminded of what it truly means to be able to see.

Owl medicine in its power animal form may also come to teach us about the two sides of who we are—the light and the dark—and how to bring them together as part of our whole being. We tend to hide aspects of ourselves that we feel others or society may not approve of. We also hide things from ourselves. This becomes our shadow self, the part of us we keep in the dark. The energy of the great horned owl might come to remind you that you can be both fierce and good-natured. Their medicine will assist you in reconciling your two halves by embracing them both.

THE OWL FOR HEALING MEDICINE

Many cultures across the world believe owls to be healers and treat them as such. Feathers are used to clear away negative energies that are thought to be causing illnesses. The Zuni people believed that an owl feather in a baby's bed would keep evil and sickness away.[44]

Many believe calling upon the power of the owl's eyes is a way to improve your own physical vision and your night vision.

It has been said that finding an owl's nest full of eggs or hatchlings will assist with any complications centered around fertility.

Seeing an owl in the daylight has been said to help with issues of insomnia.

Listening to the calming hoot of the great horned owl can promote energetic healing. Their call, which has a frequency of about 300 to 400 Hz, can help heal a variety of things including the release of root and sacral chakra blockages and trauma.[45] A

Seeking Spiritual Lessons

Use this spell to learn what your soul needs for spiritual growth.

YOU WILL NEED

- A comfortable space to sit
- A purple candle
- A cauldron or fireproof dish
- 1 teaspoon of mugwort
- Clear alcohol—Everclear works well
- Lighter or matches
- A timer (using your phone is acceptable)
- A journal
- A pen or pencil

THE WORKING

1. Go into your sacred space.
2. Place the candle, cauldron, and mugwort on your altar.
3. Cast a circle.
4. Pour a small amount of the alcohol into the cauldron.
5. Sprinkle in the mugwort, light it, and let it burn. (Remember to be careful when working with fire.)
6. Invoke the owl.
7. Light the purple candle and intone the following:

> *Owl medicine for spiritual growth,*
> *Guide me and give your oath*
> *To show me what I must address.*
> *Help to gain knowledge without duress.*
> *Let me see what my soul is seeking.*
> *I pledge to listen while you are speaking.*

8. Set the timer for 15 minutes and close your eyes.
9. Once the timer goes off, come back to yourself.
10. When you are ready, open your eyes.
11. Write down any messages you received regarding what needs to be done for your soul growth.
12. Thank the owl for their assistance and bid them farewell.
13. Open the circle.

frequency of 285 Hz has the potential to heal and restore tissue. It supports the immune system and balances your energy. The frequency of 396 Hz is said to heal guilt and other trapped feelings within the root chakra, such as subconscious fears and grief. A frequency of 417 Hz is said to aid in healing trauma and clear negative energy from the body. It can potentially counteract negative behavior patterns, encourage you to embrace change, and promote restful sleep.[34]

CALLING OWL ENERGY FOR SPIRITUAL GROWTH

Our spiritual growth within each of our lifetimes is what nurtures and teaches our souls. Owl guides and familiars come into our lives to assist us with the evolution of our souls. We might also want to call upon the energy of a different species of owl if they are better suited to the task or for targeted spiritual development.

Your first step is to find out what it is that your soul requires at the moment. You can ask your owl guide or familiar to assist you with this through the meditation spell on page 129.

WORKINGS FOR SOUL GROWTH USING OWL MEDICINE

Once you know what it is that you need to work on, you can decide how to go about it. Since most owls align with lunar energy, working with the phases of the Moon is often appropriate. Days of the week also correspond to different energies. Owl medicine will likely guide you and show you how timing can affect your plan of action. You can learn more about Moon phases and timing in the Magickal References and Tools section on page 140.

Use the knowledge you have gained in the previous chapters to assess how to call owls in a way that will be most effective for your ritual work. Is your personal magick part of how you need to grow spiritually? Asking your owl familiar or guide for their medicine to assist you with your magick is beneficial.

OWL MEDICINE WHEN SPIRITUAL AND EMOTIONAL HEALING IS REQUIRED

One of the bravest things we can do is dive into our own spiritual and emotional healing. Many times, we have spiritual or energetic issues going on that begin to manifest as physical issues within our bodies. When we begin to take control of our spiritual and emotional well-being, it has a ripple effect throughout our bodies and then our lives.

By invoking the medicine that the owl has to offer, you set yourself up for incredible healing and have a powerful ally at the ready. Remember that owl medicine can facilitate:

- Clearing out heavy energies.
- Trusting in ourselves, our intuition, and our instincts.
- Teaching us to set and maintain healthy boundaries.
- Balancing between our light and our dark.

Sometimes we need to call upon owl medicine, and other times, it shows up for us by way of messages and guides. Be open to what is showing up for you.

Remember that healing work can be difficult, so be gentle with yourself. Be aware of what comes up for you over the next few weeks. You can continue to light a white candle every week and intone the chant three times until you feel that it has taken hold.

Healing Spell with Owl Medicine

Use this spell to invoke the owl's medicine for healing.

YOU WILL NEED

- A white candle (an owl-shaped one is even better)
- A cauldron or fireproof dish
- One or two small pieces of paper
- A pen or pencil
- Lighter or matches
- A timer (using your phone is acceptable)

THE WORKING

1. Go into your sacred space.
2. Set the candle and the cauldron on your altar.
3. Cast a circle.
4. On the strip of paper, write out what it is that needs to be healed (keep to one or two things at a time so as not to be overwhelmed).
5. Invoke your owl guide or familiar.
6. Light the white candle and intone the following one time:

> *Owl medicine, I call to you.*
> *We have this work to do.*
> *Healing energy is what I need.*
> *Bring to me with gentle speed,*
> *Whether mind, body, or spirit,*
> *Owl medicine here to heal it.*

7. Say out loud what is written on the paper.
8. Light the paper and drop it into the cauldron.
9. Make sure the paper burns up completely. As always, be careful when working with open flames.
10. Let the candle burn for 9 minutes and then snuff it out.
11. Thank the owl for their assistance and bid them farewell.
12. Open the circle.
13. Dispose of the remaining candle and paper ash off of your property. A public trash can will work just fine.

If you are doing healing work for others, this spell is easy to apply to them as well.

SOUL RETRIEVAL THROUGH OWL MEDICINE

There are times in our lives, present or past, when we experience something so deeply that part of ourselves fragments and becomes disconnected. This can be something that happens in a single moment or over time, and we are typically completely aware that it is happening. When parts of our soul are missing, we can feel it on a very deep level even if we cannot pinpoint the cause. We just have a knowing that something is missing.

Soul loss is an ancient Shamanic term that best describes what happens to our energetic being when we experience trauma. Times of extreme crisis and trauma result in soul fracturing. Toxic relationships can cause a different type of soul loss with the same results.

Shamans or other spiritual healers with experience in this work are the ones typically working with this kind of healing medicine. The soul guides the Shaman in a journey to where the fractured parts are stuck, helping these pieces to find their way back to the whole. Soul parts can typically only rejoin their person once they are aware of the healing that is needed to facilitate a cohesive union.

With the help of the owl, an individual can work on their own soul retrieval. Because owls have such a deep connection to the spiritual and metaphysical realms; the ability to see into the dark, the unknown, and what has been hidden; as well as the ability to view multiple timelines and past lives at once, they are masters when it comes to soul retrieval. If you feel like you might have soul loss, call upon the owl to assist in bringing it back.

Owl Medicine for Soul Retrieval

Use this meditation work to assist you with soul retrieval.

YOU WILL NEED

- A comfortable, protected space where you will not be disturbed, such as your sacred space
- A purple candle
- A white candle
- Lighter or matches
- A timer (using your phone is acceptable)
- A journal
- A pen or pencil

THE WORKING

1. Go into your sacred space.
2. Place the purple and white candles on your altar.
3. Cast a circle.
4. Invoke the owl.
5. Light the candles and intone the following intentions:

> *I seek the owl's assistance at this time. I wish to retrieve the parts of myself, pieces of my soul that have been lost. I ask that you show me the healing that is necessary to reconcile the soul parts with their whole. Any part that is not for my best and highest good at this moment will only come back once the time is right. So mote it be.*

6. Here are the words that will set in motion the soul retrieval. Get comfortable, set the timer for 15 to 20 minutes, then read the following:

> *Defend the night*
> *Against endless days*
> *The sun too bright*
> *Longing for moon's cool light*
> *Crashing tides*
> *Fly and dive*
> *Into the abyss.*

The darkness leads astray
Those wandering in the void
Her seduction is total
And speaks right to your soul.

The darkness takes hold
Within the abyss
No way out
Lost to the torment
Of this aching soul.

The veil will fall
When dark and light collide
Past and present
Listen now
The spirits speak
Wisdom and Guidance.

The owl is sent
Taking charge
Rescuing the soul
That was thought to be lost.

7. Close your eyes and let the owl find what it is that you are seeking.
8. When the timer goes off, come back to yourself. Wiggle your fingers and toes and ground yourself.
9. When you are ready, open your eyes.
10. Write down any experiences or messages. How do you feel?
11. Thank the owl for their assistance and bid them farewell.
12. Snuff the candles, making sure all the fire is out.
13. Open the circle.

TIP ⟨ You can work for your own soul retrieval, but unless you have training in doing so for others, do not attempt this on anyone but yourself. Soul retrieval work should be left to Shamans and other spiritual healers.

RITUAL WORK WITH HEALING OWL MEDICINE

You will find invoking owl medicine into your ritual work to be extremely powerful and beautiful, but also very intimate and highly personal. For rituals, one might consider calling upon one of the deities associated with owl magick from the first chapter. You might also want to utilize other aspects of the owl and their energy for a powerful combination of owl medicine.

Moon energy is tied to our emotions and can cause powerful tides of change within them. The lunar alignment of the majority of owls may bring up strong emotional aspects for an individual when calling upon them to work a ritual. This is okay. This simply means that there is work to be done there and that the healing is beginning to take place. After all, the first step in healing is to acknowledge that there is an issue. The owl medicine will allow you to feel these emotions, learn where they are coming from, and address them in the most effective way. Be aware that sometimes owl medicine is not as gentle as we would wish it to be. Sometimes healing means ripping off the Band-Aid and examining the wound. Being in ritual when owl medicine is invoked can leave one feeling raw and exposed, but know this—the owl will not abandon you to yourself. The energy of owl medicine will stay with you as long as you need it for continued healing.

Magickal Reference and Tools

This section serves as a place of reference. Here you will find information on the magickal days of the week, Moon and Sun phases/ timing, candle magick and corresponding colors, as well as some basic herbs and crystals. All of these things can be used alongside your guide or familiar's power to strengthen spells as well as bring your magickal workings to the next level. For example, if you are working a protection spell on a Saturday using a black candle dressed with (common) sage and rosemary, the magick tied to it will be some of the most powerful available. If you want to try a communication spell with your familiar, work it on a Wednesday using a blue candle.

When we use all of our magickal knowledge and incorporate tools such as magickal timing (days of the week, Moon or Sun phases), candle color correspondences, or herbs and crystals, we might notice that it take less energy from both ourselves and our familiars to work a spell. Using this wisdom gives us the needed boost that is often required for the higher and more complex magicks without tapping into our own precious well of energy.

MAGICKAL DAYS OF THE WEEK

Each day of the week holds a specific energy. When we align our magickal working to the day that corresponds with what we are trying to achieve, it reinforces the intentions of the spell and adds power.

Sunday, The Sun's Day: Divine Masculine, success, happiness, joy, vitality, creativity, confidence

Monday, The Moon's Day: Dreams, the subconscious, intuition, scrying, divination, water magick, emotions, women's magicks, domestic issues

Tuesday, Mars's Day: Quick action, ambition, sexual potency, passion, personal strength, self-assertion, victory, protection

Wednesday, Mercury's Day: Communication, technology, focus and alertness, learning, writing

Thursday, Jupiter's Day: Luck, abundance and prosperity, increasing and preservation of wealth, business

Friday, Venus's Day: Divine Feminine, love, relationships and friendships, beauty, glamour magick, peace, harmony

Saturday, Saturn's Day: Protection, banishing and binding, communing with ancestors and departed spirits, overcoming obstacles

MOON PHASES

As witches, we are well aware of the powerful energies that the Moon holds. When we align our spells with the different Moon phases, it will further empower them with the energy of that phase. Because the owl's energy naturally syncs with the Moon, they can easily facilitate a deeper working for you.

New or Dark Moon: Setting intentions, manifestation, new beginnings, shadow work

Waxing Crescent: Nurturing, self-love, compassion, courage, positive mindset

First Quarter: Drawing things to you, such as a new job, love interest, success, money, etc.

Waxing Gibbous: Fertility, endurance, breaking through what one may be resisting

Full Moon: Release, letting go of what no longer serves us, cleansing, protection

Waning Gibbous: Minor banishings, cleansing

Last Quarter: Removing obstacles, allowing flow, breaking addictions

Waning Crescent: Major banishings, removing toxic relationships or situations

SUN TIMING

The Sun holds its own powerful energies, and we can use specific timing throughout the day to aid our spell and ritual work. We can also connect with solar owl energies such as the snowy owl and the burrowing owl that hunt during the daylight hours to help facilitate Sun magick into our workings.

- **Sunrise/dawn:** New beginnings, manifestation, hope, charging energies

- **Morning:** Growth, building, relationships, wealth

- **Noon:** Protection, justice, health, courage, success

- **Afternoon:** Clarity, resolution, business communication

- **Sunset/dusk:** Endings, release/letting go, banishment, divination

CANDLE MAGICK

Candles are commonplace materials when it comes to rituals and spell work. We use them on our altars, to create sacred spaces, to cast circles, and more. Using specific candle colors for a working can be an extremely effective way to boost the spell's power. Like most other things in witchcraft, candles hold their own vibrational patterns, and the different colors align with specific magickal workings.

Dressing a candle includes the use of an oil and herbs. Typically, a carrier oil (an oil that is paired with essential oils to dilute them, such as jojoba, sweet almond, or even olive oil) is used to anoint the candle. Anointing is simply rubbing the candle with the oil and giving it its purpose through stating the intentions of the working. The anointed candle is then rolled in dried herbs that correspond to the spell.

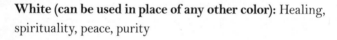

White (can be used in place of any other color): Healing, spirituality, peace, purity

Black: Protection, banishing, binding, repelling negative energies, magick (also associated with witches)

Brown: Earth energy (grounding), animals, stability, home protection, family

Red: Vitality, passion, romantic love, strength, fast action, courage, root chakra

Pink: Self-love, friendship, emotional healing, nurturing

Yellow: Happiness, joy, success, power, Sun energy, solar plexus chakra

 Orange: Creativity, expression, adventure, positivity, sacral chakra

 Green: Nature, physical healing, money (abundance and prosperity), growth, heart chakra

 Blue: Communication, inspiration, calming, throat (royal blue) and third eye (indigo) chakras

 Purple: Psychic abilities, hidden knowledge, divination, astral projection, crown chakra

 Silver: Divine Feminine, intuition, dreams, Moon energies

 Gold: Divine Masculine, wealth, luck, happiness, Sun energies

MAGICKAL HERBS

All plants have unique vibrational patterns and properties. Many of them have strong magickal energies as well as medicinal uses. The list of magickal plants is almost endless, so we'll just cover some of the basics here.

 Healing: Angelica, yarrow, echinacea, lemon balm, tansy, rosemary, horehound

 Protection: Sage, rosemary, pine, juniper, cedar, garlic, rue, nettles, angelica

 Communication: Clary sage, rosemary, bay leaf

 Love: Red (romance) and pink (self and friends) roses, lavender, vanilla, basil, jasmine

 Money: Basil, cinnamon, bay leaf, mint, juniper, cinquefoil, alfalfa

 Divination: Mugwort, rosemary, clary sage, dandelion, star anise

 Calming/sleep: Lavender, chamomile, lemon balm, bergamot, St. John's wort

 Fertility: Pine and spruce (to balance masculine and feminine), cinnamon, nettles, vanilla, willow, red and orange rose petals (to activate root and sacral chakras/sex organs)

Happiness and joy: Marjoram, lavender, St. John's wort, mint, lemon balm, pine

 Divine Feminine: Spruce, willow, motherwort, jasmine, mugwort, apple

 Divine Masculine: Pine, sunflower, mint, bay leaf, basil, St. John's wort, oak leaves

CRYSTAL CORRESPONDENCES

Crystals are powerful magickal allies. They boost our own energies and the energy of the spell. They protect, heal, and facilitate communication between our higher selves, the Universe, deities, and our guides. We can charge them for a specific purpose and carry them as a talisman. Combining their energy with other magickal tools such as herbs, candle magick, and the energy lent by your familiar will further empower your workings.

Crystals can be added to mojo or charm bags along with herbs and other magickal items for a variety of uses, including protection, sleep, money drawing, and healing. You can also create a grid with crystals for these same purposes. Crystal grids use the power of sacred geometry to combine the energies of the individual crystals you are using for a specific working. Crystal grid layouts can be easily found online. If you wanted to create a powerful grid for protection, for example, you could use the listed protection crystals along with some sage and rosemary. Include some ethically sourced owl talons for an added boost. You can ask your familiar to infuse their natural protective instincts into the grid.

 Healing: Amethyst, clear quartz, bloodstone, lepidolite, labradorite, agate, sugilite

 Protection: Black obsidian, black tourmaline, smoky quartz, labradorite, jet

 Communication: Sodalite, petalite, fluorite, blue lace agate

 Love: Rose quartz, garnet, ruby, rhodochrosite, rhodonite

Money: Jade, pyrite, goldstone, emerald, citrine, tiger's eye

 Divination: Selenite, moonstone, labradorite, petalite, lapis lazuli

 Calming/sleep: Amethyst, selenite, moonstone, aquamarine, bloodstone

 Fertility: Pink tourmaline, red/orange carnelian, moonstone, garnet, green aventurine

 Happiness and joy: Citrine, sunstone, dalmatian jasper, tiger's eye

Taking Off into the Night Again

W hen you finally make the leap, spread your wings, and take flight into the night with the owl—the sky's the limit. Owls are revered across the globe for many different reasons. They are a vital part of the ecosystem. Simply by existing as themselves, hunting the prey they feed upon to survive, birds of prey help control the rodent population. Just one species of owl disappearing and becoming extinct would be a tremendous loss to the world, not only because of the role they play in nature but because of the energy and magick they emanate. Practices of persecution against owls, including killing them for dark, magickal purposes, need to end, and this can only be done through education and conservation efforts.

There are many witches and magickal people that say they feel safer knowing they live in a world with these spiritual guardians, especially if they have an owl as a guide or familiar. As we have learned, the energy of the owl is extraordinary and powerful. Owls are our connection to the Divine as well as to higher levels of wisdom, knowledge, and learning. They are teachers, guides, familiars, and powerful medicine bringers. These beautiful raptors facilitate communication with the world of Spirit and show us how to pierce the veil when needed. They give us Sight that we might never have had on our own. Owls show us the way when we are lost in the dark.

The essence of the owl's energy alone should be enough to protect them and their environments. It is certainly one of the reasons why magickal people all over the world venerate them and associate them with deities. The importance of owls throughout history can be seen in carvings, paintings, other artwork, and mythology. Witches and Shamans alike have worked with the power of the owl for more than a millennium, knowing how special and unique these creatures are. It is only because we humans fear the night, that which we cannot see, that the owl became the villain in some stories.

The overall energy of the owl vibrates at a level that easily connects them to the world of Spirit and helps us connect with it as well on a much deeper level.

When we work with the energy of the owl, it opens up our minds and shows us things we might never have thought to question. It opens up our magick as well, showing us where we can excel and soar. Remember that even if you do not have an owl as a guide or familiar, you can still call upon them and their energy using the various information, techniques, and spells found within this book.

Choosing to take flight with the owl will be a remarkable experience. You learn to leap from the nest without fear, spread your wings, and fly into the unknown with confidence, not only in yourself, but also in your magickal practice. Learning to trust your own insight, wisdom, and intuition is one of the greatest gifts that an owl can bring to you.

So what are you waiting for? The sun is setting and the owl is calling. It's time to fly with it into the night again.

Thank You

To my longtime friend and sister of my soul, Angie, thank you for those times so long ago when you believed in me and stood by me when no one else did. I wouldn't be where I am today if not for you. I am so grateful to have you in my life. Love ya!

To my Collective, the Silver Phoenixes, thank you for your continued love and support. Lady Lumosulo, Lady Eala, Lady Rowena Hawkfeather, and Caci, I love and appreciate you all so very much.

I am grateful today and every day for my goddess-given gift of being able to communicate with animals. I am thankful for all the messengers, animal guides, and protectors.

Thank you to Quarto Publishing for the opportunity to share this knowledge with you. Thank you to the editors and the design team that put so much hard work into all the books, turning the writing into a beautiful creation.

About the Author

RIEKA MOONSONG is a Wiccan High Priestess who is currently training to become clergy. She is also an Andean tradition-trained, mesa-carrying Shaman. It is her journey, soul path, and goddess-given gift to teach, to share wisdom and knowledge with others, and to help facilitate healing and growth for those on their own journeys. She resides in Colorado with her feline familiar, Artemis.

Rieka has always felt the call to work with animals and their energies, even as a child. She currently has twenty-one animal guides, including a snowy owl, and uses her natural ability to connect with them for wisdom and guidance. It is her dream to help others form close bonds with their familiars as well as other animals, and to teach them how to call upon these energies when they are needed. *Owl Magick* is a true labor of love for her.

References

1. Wikipedia, "Owl," https://en.wikipedia.org/wiki/Owl.

2. Coastside Land Trust, "Owl Pellets," https://www.coastsidelandtrust.org/our-blog/2020/5/16/owl-pellets.

3. Wikipedia, "Owl of Athena," https://en.wikipedia.org/wiki/Owl_of_Athena.

4. Eggenberger, Sophia, "Owl of Athena on the Union Building," UTexas.edu, July 30, 2019. https://sites.utexas.edu/classicalmythutcampus/2019/07/.

5. Fields, Kitty, "Owl Goddesses Across Cultures: Athena, Ragana, and More," OtherwordlyOracle.com, August 20, 2019. https://otherworldlyoracle.com/owl-goddesses/.

6. Pekantytar Niina, "Ragana Baltic Goddess of Witches and Death" Owlcation.com, January 20, 2023. https://owlcation.com/humanities/Ragana-Baltic-Goddess-of-Witches.

7. Wikipedia, "Lilith," https://en.wikipedia.org/wiki/Lilith.

8. Knowles, George, "Animals and Witchcraft (The Witch's Familiar)," Controverscial.com. https://www.controverscial.com/Animals%20and%20Witchcraft%20-%20Owl.htm.

9. Aleeiah, "The Medicine and Mythology of Owls," ShamansMarket.com. https://www.shamansmarket.com/blogs/musings/the-medicine-and-mythology-of-owls.

10. Johnson, Terry W., "Out My Backdoor: Owls Don't Deserve Their Bad Reputation," GeorgiaWildlife.com. https://georgiawildlife.com/out-my-backdoor-owls-don%E2%80%99t-deserve-their-bad-reputation.

11. Freidman, Shani, "Owl Myths and Legends," WildBirdsOnline.com, October 12, 2016. https://wildbirdsonline.com/blogs/news/owl-myths-and-legends.

12. Wigington, Patti, "Owl Folklore and Legends, Magic, and Mysteries," LearnReligions.com, January 18, 2019. https://www.learnreligions.com/legends-and-lore-of-owls-2562495.

13. Wikipedia, "Strix (mythology)," https://en.m.wikipedia.org/wiki/Strix_(mythology).

14. Monsterpedia, "Strix," https://www.monstropedia.org/index.php?title=Strix.

15. Hardt, Braelei, "Why are Bats, Owls, Toads, and Crows Associated with Halloween?" NWF.org, October 17, 2022. https://blog.nwf.org/2022/10/why-are-bats-owls-toads-and-crows-associated-with-halloween/.

16. Wilson, Dana, "Indian Eagle Owl Rescued from Falling Prey to 'Black Magic Ritual'," WildlifeSOS.org, November 29, 2019. https://wildlifesos.org/rescue/indian-eagle-owl-rescued-from-falling-prey-to-black-magic-ritual/.

17. Mikkola, Heimo, "Owls Used as Food and Medicine and for Witchcraft in Africa," Intechopen.com, June 6, 2022. https://www.intechopen.com/chapters/85023#.

18. Wall, Kimberly, "The Fascinating Meaning of Owls in the Bible," BibleKeeper.com, November 17, 2022. https://www.biblekeeper.com/owl-meaning-in-the-bible/.

19. "How Can an Owl Catch a Mouse Under a Foot of Snow in Total Darkness?" AllAboutBirds.org. https://www.allaboutbirds.org/news/how-can-an-owl-catch-a-mouse-underneath-a-foot-of-snow-in-total-darkness/.

20. Couch, Stacey L. L., "Spirit Animals: Barn Owl" WildGratitude.com, December 11, 2014. https://www.wildgratitude.com/barn-owl-symbolism/.

21. Kayne, R., "What is Native American Animal Medicine?" LanguageHumanities.org, September 28, 2022. https://www. languagehumanities.org/what-is-native-american-animal-medicine.htm.

22. Guveya, Naume, "The Benefits of the 9 Solfeggio Frequencies," Ouraring. com, May 31, 2023. https://ouraring.com/blog/the-benefits-of-the-9-solfeggio-frequencies/.

23. "Hecate and Owls: Ancient Symbols of Wisdom and Mystery," Pagan-Workshop.com, July 23, 2023. https://pagan-workshop.com/blogs/blog/hecate-and-owls-ancient-symbols-of-wisdom-and-mystery.

24. Historian, "Owl Beliefs Among Traditional NDN People," HealthyPages. co.uk, August 25, 2008. https://www.healthypages.co.uk/community/mystical-shamanism/owl-beliefs-among-traditional-ndn-people/.

25. Hay, Anne, "Owls in Native American Culture," CenterOfTheWest.org, August 6, 2018. https://centerofthewest.org/2018/08/06/owls-native-american-culture/.

26. Lewis, Deane, "Eastern Grass Owl - *Tyto Longimembris*," OwlPages.com, September 29, 2020. https://www.owlpages.com/owls/species.php?s=220.

27. Lewis, Deane, "World Owl Mythology," OwlPages.com, October 6, 2012. https://www.owlpages.com/owls/articles.php?a=63.

28. David, Lauren, "The Spiritual Meaning Of Owls And What To Do If They Keep Appearing To You," MindGreenBody.com, November 18, 2022. https://www.mindbodygreen.com/articles/owl-symbolism.

29. Riegel, Ralph, "Campaign to Protect Barn Owl that Inspired Banshee Legend," IrishIndependent.ie, June 10, 2021. https://m.independent. ie/irish-news/campaign-to-protect-barn-owl-that-inspired-banshee-legend/40523963.html.

30. Christian Pure Team, "What Does an Owl Symbolize in the Bible? Decoding the Mystery," ChristianPure.com, December 25, 2023. https://www.christianpure.com/learn/what-does-an-owl-symbolize-in-the-bible.

31. Andrews, Candice Gaukel, "Owls Have Heads Designed for Hearing," NATHAB.org, April 9, 2019. https://www.nathab.com/blog/video-owls-have-heads-designed-for-hearing/.

32. Rowling, J. K., "Owls," WizardingWorld.com, August 10, 2015. https://www.wizardingworld.com/writing-by-jk-rowling/owls.

33. Jarvis, Kila, and Denver Holt, "About Owls," OwlRearchInstitute.org. https://www.owlresearchinstitute.org/owls-1.

34. "Barn Owl Adaptations," BarnOwlTrust.org.uk. https://www.barnowltrust.org.uk/barn-owl-facts/barn-owl-adaptations/.

35. Gilfedder, Mat, "Australian Masked-owl." PeregrineFund.org. https://peregrinefund.org/explore-raptors-species/owls/australian-masked-owl.

36. "Oriental Bay Owl," Inaturalist.org. https://www.inaturalist.org/taxa/513060-Phodilus-badius.

37. Marshall, Joe T. and Frank Gill, "Owl," Britannica.com, February 1, 2024. https://www.britannica.com/animal/owl.

38. Cholewiak, Danielle, "Strigidae Typical Owls." AnimalDiversity.org, 2003. https://animaldiversity.org/accounts/Strigidae/.

39. "Burrowing Owl Life History," AllAboutBirds.org. https://www.allaboutbirds.org/guide/Burrowing_Owl/lifehistory#.

40. Jones, Jennifer, "5 Largest Owls in the World," Largest.org, November 25, 2018. https://largest.org/animals/owls/.

41. Bodkin, James, "Common Barn-owl," PeregrineFund.org. https://peregrinefund.org/explore-raptors-species/owls/barn-owl.

42. "Snowy Owl," AllAboutBirds.org. https://www.allaboutbirds.org/guide/Snowy_Owl/overview.

43. Bear, Anthony, "Owl Medicine," BearBlend.com, January 10, 2016. https://bearblend.com/bear-blog/owl-medicine/.

44. Lyn, Sarah, "Animal Allies: Owls and the Afterlife," WalkingWithAncestors.blogspot, November 7, 2012. http://walkingwithancestors.blogspot.com/2012/11/animal-allies-owls-and-afterlife.html.

45. Kinstler, Karla A., "Great Horned Owl *Bubo Virginianus* Vocalizations and Associated Behaviors," Bioone.org, December 1, 2009. https://bioone.org/journals/ardea/volume-97/issue-4/078.097.0403/Great-Horned-Owl-Bubo-virginianus-Vocalizations-and-Associated-Behaviours/10.5253/078.097.0403.full.

Index

First published in 2024 by Rock Point,
an imprint of The Quarto Group,
142 West 36th Street, 4th Floor,
New York, NY 10018, USA
(212) 779-4972 www.Quarto.com

Rock Point titles are also available at discount
for retail, wholesale, promotional, and bulk
purchase. For details, contact the Special Sales
Manager by email at specialsales@quarto.com
or by mail at The Quarto Group, Attn: Special
Sales Manager, 100 Cummings Center Suite
265D, Beverly, MA 01915 USA.

10 9 8 7 6 5 4 3 2 1

ISBN: 978-1-63106-996-3

Digital edition published in 2024
eISBN: 978-0-7603-8831-0

Library of Congress Control Number:
2024933385

Publisher: Rage Kindelsperger
Creative Director: Laura Drew
Senior Art Director: Marisa Kwek
Managing Editor: Cara Donaldson
Editors: Keyla Pizarro-Hernández and
Katelynn Abraham
Cover Design: Marisa Kwek
Interior Layout: Wendy Lai
Illustrations: Maggie Vandewalle: cover,
4, 7, 10, 17, 34, 42, 58, 63, 76, 88, 108, 124;
Crystal Sea Studio: 18, 20, 24, 28, 30,31, 41,
45, 48, 49, 55, 61, 64, 66, 68, 70, 71, 78, 84,
87, 91, 93, 102, 111, 120, 126, 135, 141, 155;
DigitalfileGraphics: 13, 23, 39, 51, 73, 75, 90,
107, 115, 126, 143

Printed in China